THE MATCH MAKERS

PATRICK BEAVER

THE MATCH MAKERS

Henry Melland London

First published in Great Britain
by Henry Melland Limited
23 Ridgmount Street, London WC1E 7AH
1985
for Bryant & May Limited
Sword House, Totteridge Road,
High Wycombe, Bucks HP13 6EJ

Distributed by Celerity Book Service,
Sedgwick Park, Horsham, Sussex RH13 6QH

All rights reserved. No part of this
publication may be reproduced or
transmitted in any form, or by any means,
without prior permission of the
copyright owner. Enquiries should be
addressed to the publishers.

© Bryant & May Limited 1985

Designed by Maurice Rickards

ISBN 0 907929 11 7

Set in 10 on 12 point Century Schoolbook
Printed in England by
Jolly & Barber Limited, Rugby

SUPPORT HOME INDUSTRIES.

BUY
BRYANT & MAY'S
MATCHES.

TRADE MARK — SECURITY

MANUFACTURED ONLY IN THE EAST-END OF LONDON.

PATENT SAFETY MATCHES.

PROTECTION FROM FIRE.

Entirely Free from Phosphorus.   Are not Poisonous.

HARMLESS TO ALL EMPLOYED IN THEIR MANUFACTURE.

PROTECTION TO HEALTH.

THE UNEMPLOYED IN EAST LONDON.—At a time when much thought is being given to the matter, a practical suggestion may be of service. Last year more than £300,000 worth of foreign matches were purchased by inconsiderate consumers in this country, to the great injury of our own working people. So true is it that "Evil is wrought by want of thought as well as want of heart." If all consumers would purchase Bryant & May's Matches, that firm would be enabled to pay £1000 a week more in wages.

19 PRIZE MEDALS.

Price Lists for Matches and Decorated Tinware on application.

SUPPORT HOME INDUSTRIES
AND
EMPLOY BRITISH LABOUR.

The Grocer August 1982

By the same author:

The Big Ship — Brunel's Great Eastern (London 1969)

The Crystal Palace (London 1970)

A History of Lighthouses (London 1971)

A History of Tunnels (London 1972)

The Wipers Times (London 1973)

Victorian Parlour Games for Today (London 1974)

The Spice of Life — some Victorian Entertainments (London 1979)

ACKNOWLEDGEMENTS

The author wishes to thank all those of Bryant & May Limited who have given so much help in the compiling of this history: in particular, Richard Armitage, Muriel Smith and Ian Brook, for their untiring assistance. He is also indebted to Gilbert P Bartholomew, Edward Lincoln and to the staff of the Rose Lipman Library at Hackney where the bulk of the company's archives are preserved.

Special thanks are due to Rolf Christophersen of John J Masters Limited for his invaluable and willing help concerning the history of the Swedish match industry.

'A tap on the pane, the quick sharp scratch
And blue flame of a lighted match…'   (Robert Browning)

'The next thing that came out of my pocket was a box of matches. Then I saw fire, which is stronger even than steel, the old fierce female thing, the thing we all love but dare not touch.'   (G K Chesterton)

'Many a small thing has been made large by the right kind of advertising.'   (Mark Twain)

CONTENTS

Foreword	11
Introduction	13

PROLOGUE: FIRE AND FIRE MAKING

Fire in Myth and Legend	15
Early Fire Making	15
Fire by Wood Friction	16
The Fire Piston	17
The Birth of the Match	18

PART ONE: BUILDING A BUSINESS

William Bryant and Francis May	23
Carl Lundström	24
Safety Matches	28
Founding a Factory 1861	35
Match Making at Bow: 1861–63	38
The First Ten Years 1861–71	42
The Match Tax Battle 1871	47
Steady Growth 1872–83	52
A Public Company 1884–87	61
The Matchgirls' Strike 1888	64
Important Developments 1888–1901	70
Diamond Match Company 1901	74

PART TWO: YEARS OF GROWTH

Modernisation and Expansion 1902–14	79
World War I 1914–18	82
A Challenge 1919–27	86
The British Match Corporation	88
Expansion in the 1930s	91
The Kreuger Crisis 1932	92
Sir George Paton	94
World War II 1939–45	95

PART THREE: THE AGE OF TECHNOLOGY

A Difficult Period 1946–49	99
The Monopolies Commission 1949	100
Planning Ahead 1950–54	103
Diversification 1955–71	103
Wilkinson Sword – Wilkinson Match 1973	107
The Company Today	110

SWAN VESTAS 1883–1985	117
MATCH MAKING TODAY	121
BRYANT & MAY CHAIRMEN: 1884–1985	127
INDEX	128

"KEEP THE HOME FIRES BURNING"
SOLO BY OUR OPTIMISTIC PREMIER

FOREWORD

I am delighted to be writing a foreword to this history of Bryant & May — a name that has long been synonymous with matches. As this history relates, William Bryant and Francis May created a company which has always been and will continue to be in a state of progressive change. In addition to providing an essential product to millions of people throughout the world, it has also been a major contributor to the social development of British industry.

I hope you enjoy the history as much as I have. Unfortunately, it was not possible to mention by name all the employees whose dedication has created a reputation second to none in the match making industry. Nevertheless, I must take this opportunity to pay tribute to the past and present employees of Bryant & May who have made the company what it is today.

The company is proud of its great history — but it still looks to its future. With the world-wide support of its parent company, Allegheny International, it will continue to progress and achieve an exciting and profitable future.

RICHARD H. ARMITAGE
Chairman
Bryant & May Limited

"Any Cards, Matches, or Save-alls."

CRIES OF LONDON

INTRODUCTION

Man has always been a fire-making animal, and the invention of the modern match in 1827 was one of the most important stages in his development. The match did away with the age-old cumbersome, tedious methods of flame kindling and replaced them with a means of instant ignition which could be conveniently carried in the pocket.

In the modern world the match is taken so much for granted that it seems insignificant. It is, perhaps, the only artifact for which we can ask a stranger and be given it without a second thought. Yet what is given is the result of a most complex process, for making a box of matches requires highly advanced machinery and scores of different commodities. These include timber, cardboard, paper, printing-inks, wax, potassium, chlorate, sand, amorphous phosphorus, various glues, manganese, felspar, zinc oxide, sulphur, potassium dichromate and carbon black.

The firm of Bryant & May Limited entered the match business in the early days of the industry and has since branched out into many other fields, but essentially the firm remains as a maker of matches – an activity that originated thousands of years ago when man first discovered the means of making fire.

PROLOGUE: FIRE AND FIRE MAKING

Fire in Myth and Legend

Without fire there can be no heat and heat is a source of life. And not only is it essential to all life but also to all human culture, for civilisation may be said to have begun with the invention of fire making and the uses of it increased in the same ratio as civilisation itself. Man has always known of the essential nature of fire, and from the earliest times created myths to explain its origin — myths which often referred back to the time when he suffered — and sometimes died — because he did not have the means to warm himself. In these stories, fire is usually provided by a god. Thus, in Greek legend, Prometheus (literally 'forethought') is the father of the human race because by giving the divine flame he saved it from annihilation.

As a giver of warmth, the sun was early known to be of burning matter, and fire on earth was seen as the sun's earthly representative providing not only heat in the day but light to guide man through the mysteries of darkness. Fire occurs in the religious rituals of all ages in all places. It was (and is) a purifier, an appropriate medium for transmitting sacrifices to the supernatural and a symbol of the eternal spirit of life. In the Old Testament, Yahweh nearly always manifested himself as fire. In primitive religions fire could be the creative force in vegetation which was invoked by rubbing a male stick into a female stock. The alchemists saw it as one of the elements that made up the earth, one of the names of Prime Matter and the agent of transmutation from which all things derived and to which they all returned. All over the world fires are still lit at important times such as solstices and equinoxes, but especially at midwinter feasts like Hallowe'en and Christmas to assist the rebirth of the sun.

In contrast to its symbolic meanings, fire still remains related to the hearth — the centre of the home, to human warmth, the cooking of food and to hospitality. It was in pursuit of these domestic comforts that man first used fire.

Early Fire Making

Fire to warm the body — later to warm the home; fire to give light during the dark hours and to frighten off wild animals; fire to worship as a mysterious and terrifying phenomenon and in thanks for the comforts it confers. Fire for cooking, for pottery making and metal working; fire to work the great pumps that were the foundation of the steam age. Fire to power factories and locomotives, to produce coal-gas, to generate electricity, to refine oil, to send men into outer space. Fire, the essential of industry from its earliest times to the present.

No human tribe has ever been without fire and the way in which even the primitive people understand it contrasts the intelligence of man with the dullness of even the highest of the apes. Man alone makes fire and the problem of making and controlling it has occupied his mind from earliest times. This has touched the imagination of Greek and Roman thinkers. The poet Lucretius (c 95–55 BC) and Vitruvius, the first-century architect, both speculated how fire was obtained by primitive peoples. Whether early man made his first fires out of curiosity or for the utilisation of heat is not known but it is certain that he was at first dependent for his camp fires upon conflagrations that were not of his making but the result of natural energy supplied in suitable form. Lightning and lava-streams, for example, are prime causes of forest fires — as is the rubbing together of two tree branches in a high wind (which primitive method of fire making survives today). Fires kindled by any of these methods must have been utilised by man long before the time when he used his dawning intelligence to create and control what had at first been a dreadful foe to be avoided.

Today, nearly all peoples have the means to make fire at will, although there still exist tribes who make it as seldom as possible, preferring rather to keep their fires burning always and who, when travelling, carry with them a smouldering brand or some other source of flame. The pygmy people of the Andaman Islands still lack an apparent method of fire making and depend on maintenance.

Prehistoric man must have been familiar with the awful power of flying incandescent particles to start a fire, and the observation of this led to the utilisation of minerals for creating fire by percussion. Thus iron pyrites (from the Greek for *fiery*) became a convenient method of fire making when once the discovery had been made that two pieces knocked together produced sparks which, if directed towards some form of tinder, resulted in flame. Later one of the pyrites was replaced by a piece of flint, quartz or other siliceous stone, and eventually it was found that flint together with iron (and later steel) was an ideal combination. The flint and steel method of fire making survived in the form of the kitchen tinder box until the coming of the match which replaced it. Even then it survived, for the method was 're-invented' during the First World War in the form of the mechanical lighter which produces fire through the friction of steel and flint.

Fire by Wood Friction

There are three chief methods of making fire by wood friction and they have been employed in all parts of the world. Even today the method is sometimes preferred to the match when sacred or ceremonial fire is required as, for instance, by the Brahmins in India who still kindle a sacrificial fire by means of a thong drill. The essential feature of all three methods is that wood dust is produced

'Fire hidden in the veins of flint' (Virgil). An early fire steel used in the flint-and-steel method of fire making.

by the friction of one piece of wood on another, and the heat produced by the friction causes the dust to smoulder and, upon blowing, sets fire to the tinder. One of the pieces of wood is called the 'hearth' (which is stationary and of softer wood) and the other the 'saw', the 'plough' or the 'drill', depending on the means used. The three methods depend upon the direction of working the active component in relation to the grain of the wood of the hearth — sawing across the grain, ploughing along it, or drilling into it. The fire saw is still used in parts of south-east Asia and its islands, in India and in Australia.

In the fire plough method the 'plough' is pushed along a groove in the hearth and heated dust accumulates at one end of the groove where it smoulders and is applied to the tinder.

The fire drill has been used all over the world and is still employed in some countries. In Europe it was used in neolithic times and survived until well after the invention of the match. It was known in ancient Egypt where it was represented as a hieroglyph, and was the chief means of fire making in many parts of Africa until recent times. In its simplest form the apparatus consists of a cylindrical or tapering drill which is rotated by hand or mechanically in a shallow pit in the hearth and, as in the other wood friction methods, the smouldering wood dust sets the tinder ablaze. There are three methods of working the fire drill mechanically, the thong drill, the bow drill and the pump drill.

Kindling fire by friction with a fire drill. The hand-rotated drill produces smouldering wood dust which ignites the shreds of tinder. This method is still used by some primitive peoples.

The Fire Piston

Originating in south-east Asia, the fire piston is a remarkable invention insofar as the prerequisite principles necessary for its invention were unknown to primitive people. It is probable that the discovery was an accident resulting from the use of some commonly-used appliance observed by a single, alert individual who was able to repeat the process.* In Europe the fire piston probably evolved from the use of some apparatus used for the compression of air, though not for fire making.

The fire piston of south-east Asia consists of a hollow cylinder of bamboo, wood or horn, closed at one end with a closely-fitting piston, the lower end of which is wrapped with thread or fibre to make a tight fit. Tinder is placed in the cylinder and the piston struck hard to force it rapidly to the bottom of the cylinder. The resulting compression of air produces heat which lights the tinder.

For thousands of years the application of heat to tinder was the only method of fire making known to man until, in Europe, various necessities demanded a simpler, more efficient and portable means of providing fire. It is interesting to trace and compare the development of modern fire-making devices with the increasing demand for fire as the industrial revolution progressed to create the technological age in which we live.

*It was through such an accident that the friction match was invented in 1827.

The Birth of the Match

The ancestor of the modern match was a wooden splint tipped with sulphur that readily ignited from the glowing tinder of the tinder box. It is not known when this device was invented but the use of it was first recorded in 1530. Then, in 1669, the German alchemist Brand (in his search for the philosopher's stone) obtained an element that was unknown in any form before his time. By boiling urine he produced a white, waxy, highly inflammable substance that glowed in the dark, and took fire in air at 34°F, which he called 'phosphorus' (from the Greek for *light-bringer*) and thus made possible for the first time the production of fire by non-mechanical means.

Although the element was used in several briefly-popular fire-producing forms, it was not applied to matches until 1680. In that year the London chemists Godfrey Haukwitz and Robert Boyle marketed coarse sheets of paper coated with phosphorus together with sulphur-tipped wooden splints which, when drawn through the paper, burst into flame.* Being very expensive, this device was not a commercial success.

No further interest was taken in phosphorus as a flame-kindler for some 80 years, during which time the civilised world continued to rely on flint, steel and tinder for the fires it needed. Then, in the latter part of the 18th century, the rapid spread of pipe and cigar smoking brought about a revived demand for phosphorus lighting devices: one such was advertised in a London newspaper in 1766:

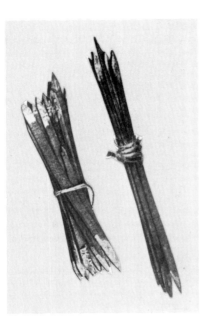

The ancestor of the modern match. A bundle of 8-inch sulphur matches. These were of deal or pine, the ends pointed and dipped in sulphur and ignited by the glowing tinder of the tinder box. They were first recorded in 1530.

> To the curious and those in particular that love to smoke a pipe in a rural situation such as fishing or any other diversion whatever. The newly invented phosphorus (*sic*) which far excels anything yet made public; extremely useful for gentlemen at sea or any person on water, where they have no fire, as two or three corns put upon a bit of paper will in half a minute light a match and about eight or nine corns put upon a pipe of tobacco will light it directly; very good for any gentleman or lady to have in their bed chamber to light their candle with when they please without trouble or the noise of striking a light. To be had at one shilling a phial which will last a long time and almost as cheap as tinder, at Mr Taille's, perfumer, the corner of Air Street, Piccadilly.

Another phosphorus fire-making gadget appeared in 1781 under the name of the 'Phosphoric Candle' or 'Ethereal Match'. This consisted of a small roll of paper tipped with phosphorus and sealed in a glass tube which, when the latter was broken (usually with the teeth), admitted air which set the paper alight. A range of similar devices, was sold by a Mr Barrett, 'wax chandler to their Majesties', and advertised as: 'Travelling Illuminators and Torch Lights by which, with the use of Philosophical Wax matches, every person may be accommodated with an immediate light on the road or in the chamber'.

---

*In principle, this was the predecessor of the modern safety match.

A small step towards the friction match was made in 1786 by the invention in Italy of the 'Pocket Luminary': this was a small bottle lined with oxide of phosphorus. Sulphur-tipped matches ignited when rubbed on this coating and withdrawn. Then in 1805 the 'Instantaneous Light Box' became popular despite the hazard of its use. This was a small bottle filled with sulphuric acid and sold with a quantity of splints, called 'Oxymurated Matches', tipped with a composition of potassium chlorate, sugar and gum-arabic which ignited when dipped in the acid. This composition was very similar to that used in the making of the first real friction match 22 years later.

The last of the early chemical fire-making devices worthy of note involved the ignition of a fine jet of hydrogen gas by an electric spark from a piece of charged resin. This foreshadowed the modern device for lighting gas-stoves and fires. The hydrogen method was developed by the German chemist Johann Dobereiner who produced a gadget which created its own gas by the action of sulphuric acid on zinc and directed it in a thin stream upon a platinum sponge to produce flame.

The first really practical friction matches were made and marketed in 1827 by John Walker, a 'chymist and druggist' of 59 High Street, Stockton-on-Tees. Walker was fond of experimenting with explosive mixtures for making percussion caps for cartridges, and

A fine example of the 'instantaneous light box' (length 3¾ inches) in japanned tin inlayed with mother-of-pearl. Within are three compartments for a small bottle of sulphuric acid, a quantity of 'oxymutated matches' and a candle.

'The greatest boon to mankind in the 19th century.' (Herbert Spencer on the friction match.) Sample of John Walker's 'friction lights' together with the record of their first sale on 7th April 1827.

Science Museum

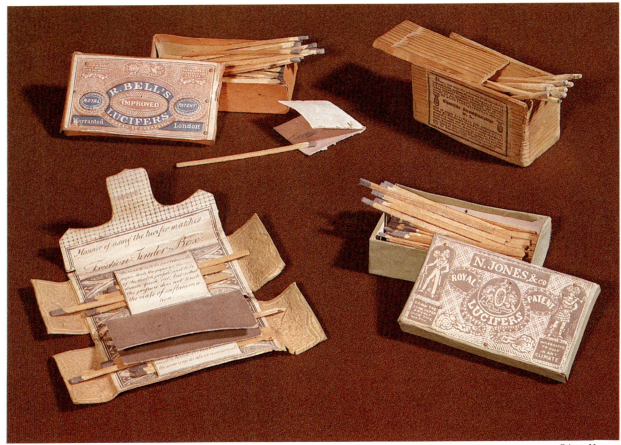

Science Museum

Lucifers and congreves. Four examples of early matches. TOP, LEFT TO RIGHT *Bell's lucifers (1833) with sandpaper for ignition. (Bell was the first manufacturer to devote himself exclusively to matches.) German congreves by H Link of Schuttenhofen (1835).* BOTTOM *Dutch lucifers for the English market (1832). N Jones' lucifers (1831) – copies of John Walker.*

it was as a result of one of these experiments that he made an accidental discovery. After combining together potassium chlorate, antimony sulphide, gum-arabic and water, he wiped his mixing stick on his hearthstone and, to his astonishment, saw it burst into flame. He at once realised that he had hit upon the thing which chemists had been seeking for some 200 years — a handy-to-carry, easily-ignitable match. He developed his discovery into what he called the 'friction match' and in so doing founded the match industry as it is today.

Walker's first sale of friction matches is recorded in his day book for 27th April 1827. It is for 100 'Sulphurata Hyperoxygenata Frict.' (the name Walker gave to his matches to disguise the formula) to a Mr Hixon for the sum of 1s 2d (6p). They were later sold at 10d for 84 plus 2d for the tin. Walker recorded every sale of friction matches and from his day book may be seen how the invention took on with the public. He sold 1,836 tins in 1827 and within three years the number increased to over 12,000. According to the day book a number of sales were made to 'young men'. This refers to the fact that at that time boys often purchased matches to ignite and throw at the feet of ladies to startle them.

Walker's matches were three-inch-long splints tipped with his mixture bound with starch, and were ignited by being drawn through a fold of glass-paper. Chemically they were excellent but needed so much friction for ignition that the head frequently wore away before a light was obtained. However, they were practical devices based on a principal that was to survive into modern times.

Phosphorus friction matches, first introduced commercially in 1833, appeared almost simultaneously in several different places and were known as 'lucifers'* or sometimes as 'congreves' after the inventor of the military rocket. They heralded their coming with burnt fingers and, often enough, burnt homes, for when struck they sent off a shower of sparks like a firework display. The gases they gave off were so noxious that one maker, Samuel Jones of the Strand, thought it wise to label the boxes with a warning: 'If possible avoid inhaling the gas that escapes from the combustion of the black composition. Persons whose lungs are delicate should by no means use the Lucifer.'

There were other dangers attendant on the use of the early phosphorus matches. Any sharp knock or jar might ignite them, and boxes left on window sills in the hot sun could burst into flame. The phosphorus itself was a deadly poison which caused a severe form of necrosis, or destruction of tissue, which was to exact a fearful toll of life among match makers for some 80 years. In addition, many persons, babies especially, were poisoned by ingesting match heads, and the phosphorus furnished an easily available source of poison for suicide — and even murder.

But with all the splutter and smell, the destruction and disease that it could cause, the friction match had come to stay, and by 1850 the once-expensive novelty had become an essential even for the poor. They were cheap even by mid-19th-century standards, as Henry Mayhew points out:

A box of congreves (1833) – the first phosphoric matches to be made commercially. This German example carries instructions for the user: 'These matches . . . must, as the above drawing shows, be taken between two fingers, and the box, being previously shut again, they may be instantly ignited by softly rubbing against the bottom of the box itself, although the same effect is produced by softly rubbing them against any other hard substance.'

> It is one of the employments to which boys, whom neglect, ill-treatment, destitution, or a vagrant disposition, have driven or lured to a street life seem to resort to . . .
>
> The trifling capital required to enter into the business is one cause of its numbering many followers. The 'fuzees', as I most frequently heard them called, are sold at the 'Congreve shops' and are chiefly German made. At one time, indeed, they were announced as 'German tinder'. The wholesale price is $4\frac{1}{2}$d [2p] per 1,000 'lights'. The 1,000 lights are apportioned into 50 rows, each of 20 self-igniting matches; and these 'rows' are sold in the streets, one or two for $\frac{1}{2}$d, and two, three or four 1d. It is common enough for a juvenile fuzee-seller to buy only 500; so that $2\frac{1}{4}$d supplies his stock in trade. The boys . . . frequent the approaches to the steamboat piers, the omnibus stands, and whatever places are resorted to by persons who love to smoke in the open air.**

This was written during the same year in which two Quakers, William Bryant and Francis May, went into the match business.

**Lucifer*: literally 'light-bringer'.

**Henry Mayhew, *London Labour and the London Poor* (1851).

PART ONE

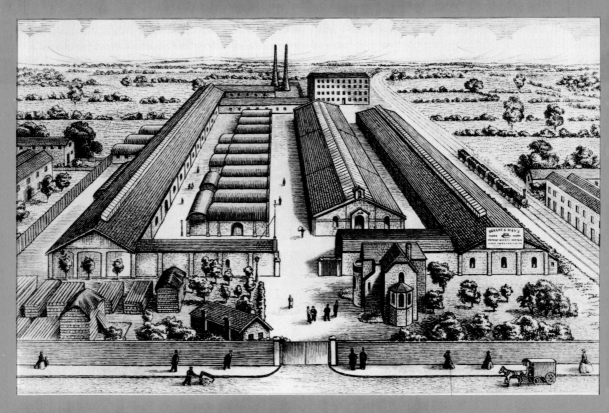

The Bryant & May match factory at Bow in the 1860s. Then on the edge of London's 'green belt' it was conveniently served by the railway. It was the first large match factory in Britain and for many years a model of its kind.

BUILDING A BUSINESS

William Bryant and Francis May

William Bryant was born in 1804, the youngest of the four children of James Bryant, a starch maker of Tiverton in Devon. During William's childhood the family moved to Plymouth where James founded a starch factory in Mill Lane. At the age of 15, William obtained employment with the Plymouth office of the Excise Service where he remained for 13 years. The Bryant family were Wesleyan Methodists but in 1832 William joined the Society of Friends. During the same year he married Ann Jago Carkeet who was of a well known Quaker family. In 1835 he went into partnership with an Edward James and together they started a firm of general merchants in Woolster Street. This business prospered and grew and in 1844 it was joined by one Burnell. Later, the firm established a soap factory in Plymouth's Coxside (now Sutton Road).

William Bryant

Bryant and James were the inventors and patentees of 'Improvements in the Manufacture of Liquid and Paste Blacking by the introduction of India Rubber, Oil and other articles and things' and it is probable that the marketing of this blacking established the first business contact between William Bryant and Francis May in about 1840.

Born in 1803, Francis May was the fourth son of Samuel May, a prosperous merchant and a member of an old Quaker family. In 1822 he began a three-year apprenticeship with a grocer at Epping and on completing it in 1824 he started on his own account as a tea dealer and grocer at 20 Bishopsgate Without in the City of London. The following year he married Jane Holmes who already had a small daughter. They eventually produced another eight children, six of whom were sons.

Francis May

There are no records to show how Francis May became associated with William Bryant but it can be presumed that as Bryant's business expanded, wider markets were sought after and it would be logical that May, a member of the Society of Friends and a prosperous City grocer, should be chosen as the agent for the West Country firm's products. Thus, the London directories for the years 1844–47 describe Francis May as 'sole consignee for Bryant & James' Patent India rubber oil and blacking'. But however the business association came about, it developed rapidly and the Bishopsgate firm expanded. In 1843 the two men entered into partnership and established the firm of Bryant & May, provision merchants, of 133–4 Tooley Street and 5 Philpot Lane. Then in 1850 occurred an event which, insignificant as it was at the time, had consequences of considerable moment on the prosperous but relatively small company of Bryant & May.

Carl Lundström

In 1850 the match-making industry in Britain was confined to a number of small factories each employing up to a dozen or so workers producing matches which for the most part were of indifferent quality. The bulk of matches sold were imported from Germany, Austria and Sweden where large match factories existed. One of the biggest Swedish factories was founded in 1848 at Jönköping by the brothers Carl and Johan Lundström.

In the autumn of 1850 Carl Lundström visited England to introduce his matches in competition with the German and Austrian products. He took with him various loose samples, two whole cases of capsules of matches and two of the boxes* to show the appearance of his bulk production and to demonstrate the consistency of its quality. He visited all the principal match importers but was unable to obtain satisfactory terms. In his memoirs he says:

> I visited them one after another and, although they all agreed that the price was not too high, none of them would buy outright; they were only willing to sell on a commission basis, in which they expected to do considerable business at a good profit, and they wanted large consignments sent over immediately. In particular, the largest firm of importers in the United Kingdom at that time were so persistent in their assurances of vast and profitable transactions that I should certainly have been caught, had it not been strongly impressed upon me during my time at Gothenburg that selling through commission houses was to be avoided as being the worst method of business. If I had listened to their arguments I should undoubtedly have suffered considerable losses for, although that firm was then considered financially sound, it was not long before they went bankrupt.

Carl Lundström, the Swedish match maker who sold Bryant & May their first consignment of matches.

Lundström then proceeds to describe his meeting with William Bryant and Francis May:

> ... as I could not obtain any more addresses from my correspondent... I decided to make enquiries at the customs office. There I met a young man who received me kindly saying that he would look into the matter and that, meanwhile, he remembered one such firm who were reputed to be particularly fair and honest and whom he considered should be highly recommended; this was Bryant & May of 133 Tooley Street.
> I set off at once and met Mr Francis May, an elderly gentleman and, judging from his clothing, a Quaker. His face, beaming with kindness and benevolence, and the friendly reception he gave me, immediately made a particularly good impression. He examined the samples with much interest and said he would recommend his partner to give our product a trial ... After he had talked matters over with his partner, Mr Bryant (a rather stiff man of dignified appearance), they asked to be allowed to examine the large cases; these they purchased and in two or three days they were to decide what quantity to order.

*Each case held 50 gross capsules (or boxes) of 100 matches each *ie* 720,000 matches.

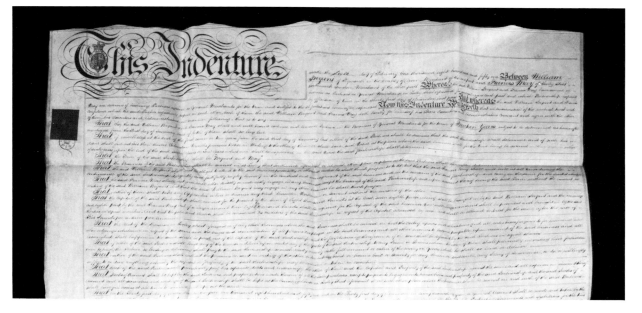

First agreement between William Bryant and Francis May whereby, in 1843, they entered into partnership for 14 years.

The next time I called on Bryant & May they ordered a small consignment, perhaps 10 or (at the most) 15 cases of 50 gross. I certainly thought it was a small order in comparison with the hundreds of cases other importers had talked about. But I was firmly convinced thay they would soon require larger consignments when the goods had time to become known, and Bryant & May themselves shared these views.

Lundström's expectations were soon realised, for shortly after the first shipment, Bryant & May ordered about double the quantity and from then larger and larger consignments until orders were never for less than 50 cases at one time. After a year or two it was not unusual for orders to be for up to 500 cases.

Thus, as will be seen, an almost chance meeting and a small order for Swedish matches led to the growth and development of an obscure London mercantile house into the international firm of Bryant & May as it is today. In the light of the success of their match venture, the partners decided to merge their respective interests into one company. Bryant was to continue to operate the Plymouth factories while May ran the London business. By the terms of a new agreement, signed in February 1851, Bryant contributed £7,000 of new capital and May £1,000.

At first the business between London and Jönköping was reciprocal, with the Lundströms selling matches to Bryant & May and the latter selling various products to the Lundströms. These included large quantities of uncut wax taper for the manufacture of vestas.* By 1851 Bryant & May were virtually sole British agents for the Jönköping factory, but their sole rights were not acknowledged until February 1854 when Carl Lundström wrote to

---

*Matches made with waxed taper, rather than wood. They are still popular in some European countries.

Johan Lundström, inventor of the first practical safety match.

report that he had received an enquiry from Charles Kuhn of Bishopsgate and saying he had replied that his matches were only sold to Bryant & May in England and that Kuhn should contact them. The Lundströms were careful to respect Bryant & May's sole rights and throughout the whole correspondence only one disagreement is recorded.

This was in May 1863 when one of the partners discovered at London docks a shipment of Jönköping matches which was not consigned to them. Bryant at once wrote indignantly to the Lundströms and received a reply which admitted the consignment, but saying it had been despatched by their forwarding agent without their knowledge. Bryant & May accepted this explanation but added severely: 'We trust you will take steps to see that such a thing cannot occur again.' The correspondence between the two firms was, on the whole, most cordial although a difference can be seen between Francis May's genial manner of writing and the sterner style of Bryant. There were, unavoidably, some differences of opinion concerning prices and conditions of payment, and it was always Bryant who dealt with such matters.

Johan Lundström visited London in the autumn of 1851 and both partners were favourably impressed by his personality. Nevertheless they found Carl more businesslike and sometimes were irritated by Johan's pretences and promises and his unwillingness to provide clear information on questions of output and deliveries. But despite occasional upsets in the course of their business, a close friendship grew between the principals, especially concerning Francis May and Carl Lundström. The brothers were frequently in London and were usually lodged and entertained by May at his Reigate home. Presents were often exchanged as well as such warm letters as the one written by May to Carl Lundström at Christmas 1855:

> Another year of our commercial connection with thee is nearly terminated, as far as we are concerned, we may say, very agreeably. We trust it has been to the mutual satisfaction and, whilst pursuing our business concerns thus pleasantly, a mutual interest has been, we believe, growing; it is a practical illustration of Free Trade cementing a kindly feeling between brethren of other nations and other creeds. May the coming year be one of increased happiness in the most important sense and of prosperity to thee and thine, thy brother and all thy friends and should life be spared to us all, may we at the end find our interest in each other's welfare increased by the increase of time. We are thy friends, Bryant & May.

The visiting and socialising was not one-sided, for in 1858 the partners visited the Lundströms at Jönköping. Soberly dressed in their Quaker clothes, they arrived in July for a visit that was not as sombre as their appearance. The feast they gave to the workers of the Jönköping factory must have been of gargantuan proportions to judge from what was left over. This included 67 bottles of port, two hams and 52 packets of coffee.

Match capsule c1860 containing about 75 round matches (length $2\frac{1}{4}$ inches).

During the first year of trading with the Lundströms, Bryant & May imported 142,848 capsules and 88,120 boxes of matches but from the following year onward they bought only boxes, the capsules having proved unpopular. The phenomenal success of the enterprise can be seen in the sales records of the first 11 years of trading.

1850	230,968	capsules and boxes
1851	1,780,500	boxes
1852	2,116,800	,,
1853	5,208,168	,,
1854	8,613,892	,,
1855	10,754,262	,,
1856	13,013,424	,,
1857	11,707,548	,,
1858	15,448,032	,,
1859	20,869,560	,,
1860	27,922,788	,,

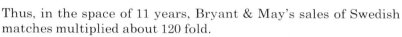

A large box containing 240 'strike anywhere' matches imported from the Lundströms by Bryant & May in the 1850s. The pink labelled wooden box measures $2\frac{3}{4} \times 2\frac{1}{2} \times 1\frac{1}{4}$ inches.

Thus, in the space of 11 years, Bryant & May's sales of Swedish matches multiplied about 120 fold.

To begin with the contents were 110 per box, but this was reduced in 1852 to 90, which drew from Bryant one of his rare letters in which 'you' is substituted for his usual 'thou'. From this letter it would appear that not satisfied with reducing the contents of the boxes, the Lundströms were proposing a price increase: 'If you expect to be able to raise your price and increase the sale at the same time you will find yourselves mistaken.'

Also in 1852 the Lundströms started to make their match boxes of wood rather than cardboard, but Bryant & May objected that the increase in weight would greaten freight charges. In the event the difference was offset by the reduction of content in each box.

The substantial extent of the yearly increase in the rate of sales was not anticipated by either side and the orders placed were never adequate to satisfy demand. In March 1853 Bryant & May reported that their stock was 'entirely sold out' and demanded further supplies. At the end of that year they made, for the first time, an estimate of their requirements for the following year which was put at 'the tremendous figure' of 7.2 million boxes. In the event, 8,613,892 boxes were sold but even that figure did not fully supply the demand, which was such that the Lundströms came to an understanding that Bryant & May could have first call on the whole of the factory's export output which, in 1856, was estimated at 14.5 million boxes.

Yet still the British demand continued to outstrip the Jönköping production capacity and, to enable the Lundströms to increase output, Bryant & May put capital into the Swedish company; this was done by purchasing a shareholding and taking up a mortgage on the factory. Even then the Lundströms could not keep up with demand and this was one of the factors which later decided the partners to build their own match factory in London. But the most important reason behind this decision was the invention by Johan Lundström in 1852 of the first practical safety match.

Safety Matches

In the years following John Walker's invention of the friction match, constant research went on to produce matches which struck only on a specially prepared surface. Then, in 1845 red (or amorphous) phosphorus was discovered. This had the advantage over the ordinary phosphorus that it did not fume or take fire in air. At first, attempts were made to include the chemical in the head of the match but, owing to the lack of sensitivity of the composition and the high cost of production, its use in this manner was found impracticable.

The problem was solved in 1852 when Johan Lundström devised a formula in which chlorate of potash was included in the match-head composition while amorphous phosphorus was added to the friction paint applied to the rubbing surface of the box. For reasons which are not clear, Johan Lundström did not patent his invention until 1855 but when he did so he sold the British patent rights to Bryant & May for the very modest sum of £100. On 15th August Francis May took out a British patent for the invention:

> I, Francis May, of Tooley Street, Southwark, Merchant, do hereby declare the nature of the Invention for Improvements in Obtaining Instantaneous Light to be as follows:–
>
> This Invention has for its object the manufacture of instantaneous matches and of the rubbing or friction surfaces employed to ignite them. The matches are manufactured in such a manner that they are not liable to ignition when subjected to simple mechanical friction, and the rubbing or friction surfaces are prepared with chemical matters in addition to the grit employed.
>
> For these purposes the matches are, by preference, dipped in sulphur or stearine, and are then tipped with a composition consisting of chlorate of potash, sulphuret of antimony, and glue, and the rubbing or friction surfaces are coated with a compound composed of grit and cement, mixed with a chemical matter for acting on and igniting the match; the chemical matter which I prefer to employ being composed of amorphous phosphorus, oxide of manganese, and glue.

First British patent for safety matches, registered by Francis May in 1855.

Having thus secured sole rights to the safety match in the United Kingdom, Bryant & May were anxious to get the article on the market without delay and they ordered a large consignment for immediate delivery. However, the Lundströms found that demand for ordinary phosphorus matches was so heavy that it was impossible for them to go into large-scale production of safeties. Therefore, it was not until the spring of 1856 that they managed to send a consignment to London – and even this was a small one, so small that Bryant & May, not wishing to whet the public appetite with a novelty they could not supply, put it in store at Tooley

Street. They did, however, begin to promote the product and informed the Lundströms of this in a letter:

> We shall get a notice of them in various Journals but we must at once turn our attention to the manners of bringing them out, we are convinced one form should be very neat and full size for the upper classes, and if thou thoughtest well to get up something very tasty and pretty we might get it presented to Prince Albert and probably obtain some useful notices from him. It is of the utmost importance to try and get rid of the spitting of the composition and prevent sparks flying off.
>
> We must turn our joint attention to the best mode of introduction throughout the country, we had thought of proposing three or four boxes being sent to various first class daily papers asking them to notice them in an early edition of their papers, if we act vigorously we hope to get out a fair quantity of the large sized boxes – it will be needful on these boxes to have our name and address as sole importers and we further think the label should be of such a character and value as to prevent any small man to imitate it, this is of much importance as men of no means will be likely to try to pirate the invention, an elaborate, expensive label would guard us and the public from imposition and would be cheap in the long run.

But despite their enthusiasm, the partners waited in vain for further supplies of safety matches until in May 1857 Bryant began to show signs of impatience. 'We feel ourselves in an entirely false position in reference to the patent matches', he wrote to Carl Lundström. A full year passed after this letter before a shipment of 20 cases arrived at London. These joined the earlier consignment in the Tooley Street store and Bryant & May ordered another 20 cases 'in order to strike while the iron is hot'. Four months after this letter the order had not been filled, and Bryant wrote again saying 'We suppose the patent match is thrown aside.' It certainly seemed so, for in March 1858 Bryant was still writing dejected letters to Carl Lundström: 'Thou dost not allude to the Patent Match. How does the case stand in reference to that article? Is it given up? We are tired of alluding to it but having gone to so much trouble and expense with it, we are mortified in the result.'

Eventually, in the autumn of 1858, eight cases were delivered but, despite pressure from London, the Lundströms would not commit themselves to regular deliveries and without that commitment Bryant & May dared not work up a market. The correspondence dragged on. In January 1859 Bryant wrote: 'The patent match we are anxious to have some certain information about, as we are convinced something should be done with it or we shall have introductions of a similar article and lose the patent altogether.'

In the following month he was reduced to pleading:

> Whilst we are desirous that nothing should interfere with a full and regular supply of the present Match [*ie*, the strike-anywhere match] and we hope you have made your arrangements for manufacturing at least 100 Cases p/week, we think it again necessary to refer you to the Patent Match and to enquire what are your views as to your enabling us to commence sale of them *during the present Spring*: we are strongly of the opinion that it would answer your purpose to make

> strenuous efforts to accomplish this and if you could only produce one or two thousand gross per month for the first year we would endeavour so to arrange as to restrain the demand until the means of supply could keep pace with it. Having taken so much pains to prepare the public mind for it we are very desirous of performing that which we have now for 2 or 3 years led them to expect in reference to this description of a match which, if much longer deferred we feel amounts to something like a want of good faith on our part and we hope your reply will release us of all apprehension on this score.

In November Bryant wrote ominously that 'one or two parties are trying to introduce a match on our patent principle that we shall lose all benefit from the article.' Later in the month the partners lost all patience and gave a first hint that they were themselves considering the manufacture of the safety match:

> We have now abandoned the idea of you giving any further attention to the manufacture of the patent match, indeed we should not wish or expect you to do so, so long as you can fully employ yourself with the present description – but under these circumstances and seeing we have for so long a time led our friends to expect a match of this kind we have thought you would be willing to give us permission and such information as might enable us to get some made in this country so that we might so far as it lies in our power to keep faith with the public.

Even this did not stop Carl Lundström's prevarications, for he replied: 'As to the patent safety match, we cannot give you any decided answer before Mr J E Lundström is returned home, which we expect in a few days.' The few days stretched into weeks with still no hint of the Lundströms' intentions on the subject of safeties. On the last day of 1859 Bryant wrote again — this time in a tone of desperation:

> We enquired about the patent whether thou wouldst allow us free use of it or on what terms thou wouldst offer us the right — I shall be glad to hear from thee on the subject — it is useless to stop others introducing the article if we don't intend to supply the British public with them. . . . let me know how I am to act by return of post.

Neither did this produce a straight answer. On 25th January 1860, Francis May took a hand with a personal letter to Carl Lundström:

> I am also sorry that thy brother does not turn his attention to the subject of the Patent after all I have endeavoured to do to serve him I feel neglected personally, if there is anything that interferes with arrangements being made, he may safely tell *me* what they are. I am placed in a very awkward position with applications from other makers to introduce the patent principle into this market, do ask him to write me fully and candidly about it.

But candour was not one of Johan Lundström's strong points, as May well knew, and it would appear that he also knew of something which, indeed, was interfering with 'arrangements', for six months later (and almost exactly five years after the registration of the British patent) Bryant wrote to Johan Lundström: 'Hast

OPPOSITE *Vesuvians, flamers, fusees, perfumed matches etc. A selection from the many brands produced at Fairfield Works in the early years.*

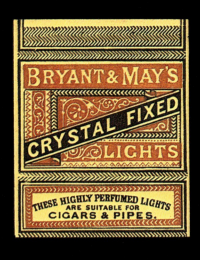
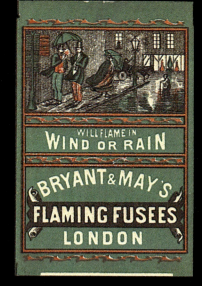

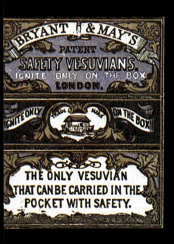

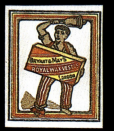

thou informed Coignet of our having purchased the Patent?' In this lies the probable key to the puzzle of the Lundströms' extraordinary reluctance to supply safety matches to Bryant & May.

For five years the brothers had equivocated with vague, ambiguous replies to Bryant & May's pressing enquiries, leaving the partners bewildered as to the cause of the delays. By 1860 the Jönköping factory was producing more than enough safety matches to fill the Swedish demand and with capacity to spare, yet its biggest export customer received only three small consignments during the entire period. The reason for this may have been the relationship which existed between Johan Lundström and the French match importers, Coignet Père & Fils of Lyons.

During a visit to France in the winter of 1855, Johan Lundström sold the French patent rights of his safety match to Coignet for a large sum in francs and the promise of a larger sum after a certain time. But before the second amount became due for payment, Coignet started proceedings against Lundström in the French courts for the return of his money on the grounds that the invention was known before. Rightly or wrongly, the court decided in Coignet's favour and adjudged him not only free from all further commitments on this account, but also entitled to a refund of what he had already paid. This sum could not be obtained from Sweden but, from that moment, Johan Lundström never set foot in France again. He was even afraid that Coignet would distrain on his luggage — which most probably would have happened. As the Swedish historians Cederschiöld and Feilitzen observed:

> Johan's fundamental reasoning concerning Bryant & May is by no means clear and it is hardly possible to explain the chain of events otherwise than on the assumption that the proceedings started by Coignet in Paris must have given Johan some form of phobia or distaste for safeties — at least outside Sweden. It is quite possible that this weak point was a contributory reason why he soon grew tired of matches altogether and took up paper manufacture.*

And there is further mystery concerning the safety match issue. The sum paid by Coignet for the French patent rights was a considerable one, and yet Lundström had earlier sold the British rights to Bryant & May for a mere £100. This, plus the Lundströms' willingness to assist Bryant & May in manufacturing safeties in London, points to the existence of some prior agreement between the two firms, the terms of which remain unknown.

But whatever the reasons for the Lundströms' strange behaviour in the matter of safety matches, it had far-reaching consequences in deciding Bryant & May to becoming match manufacturers.

Box of Bryant & May 'braided lights' first produced in about 1865. These 'wired' matches gave no flame but a smouldering fire suitable for lighting cigars.

*The History of the Swedish Match Industry.

OPPOSITE *Transient labels, reflecting current popular interest.*

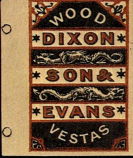

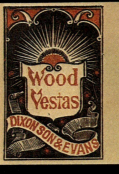

Founding a Factory

In 1860 total match production per year in the United Kingdom was some 8,000 million boxes of which two-thirds were made in London where 29 factories were operating. Most of these were so small as hardly to be factories at all but rather 'cottage industries'. Given the basic knowledge of how a match was made, it was in those days a simple matter to start a match factory. No licence was required and there was little or no government control of workers' welfare, fire precautions, *etc*. Hardly any equipment was required and the match-making process could be, and often was, carried out in the back room of private dwellings. Labour was all too plentiful and could be obtained for five shillings or less for a 60-hour week. Typical of the smaller of these establishments was the manufactory of William Adams of Princes Court in north-east London. This was in a private house and employed three girls making match boxes in a gloomy attic, a 10-year-old boy filling frames with splints and in the kitchen the proprietor dipping vesuvians.*

In David White's factory in Mile End five boys, aged between six and 17, worked in an atmosphere heavy with the fumes of phosphorus without washing or toilet facilities. Most of the other works were much the same and many of the children employed were already showing signs of phosphorus necrosis, or as it was known, 'phossy jaw'.

*Vesuvians, or 'fusees' were large matches headed with a mixture of charcoal, saltpetre, scented bark, glass and gum, tipped with phosphorus. When lighted they formed a glowing, flameless mass suitable for lighting cigars and pipes.

Match-box making at home – sweated labour that still remains a black spot on British industrial history. Hand workers could earn up to 2d ($\frac{3}{4}$p) an hour – out of which they had to provide their own paste.

OPPOSITE *Other contemporary events and interests exploited for sales promotions.*

Strip of cardboard fusees on thin deal backing c1850.

Matters were not handled in that manner in Sweden, where there were many large match factories, and pains were taken to ensure that working conditions were as healthy and pleasant as possible. This had been noticed by Bryant & May on their visits to the Lundströms' factory and they decided to use it as a model for their own: in fact, they persuaded Johan Lundström to design it for them.

In September 1860 the Bryant & May Tooley Street headquarters were moved to Whitechapel and from there a search was started for suitable factory premises. The property chosen was in Fairfield

Packing matches at Bryant & May c1880. Working conditions were grim by modern standards but a vast improvement on the average at the time.

Tower Hamlets Library

Road, Bow, a three-acre site containing the disused factories of a candle company, a crinoline maker and a rope works. Johan Lundström provided drawings for adapting the site and buildings. He also sent some of his own technicians to advise on machine installation.* From the time of its conversion to match making, Fairfield Works (as it became known) was in an almost continual state of enlargement and rebuilding and it soon became famous as a model of its kind. The factory was initially designed for the sole

*This is further evidence of some form of agreement between the two firms.

Wilberforce Bryant

Arthur Bryant

manufacture of safeties, while phosphorus matches were still obtained from Jönköping. During the first years of operation 'splints' (match sticks) and boxes for safeties were also imported from Sweden. Fairfield Works opened in July 1861 for the manufacture of 'Patent Safety Matches and other Chemical Lights'.

The move into match making changed the whole complexion of the business of Bryant & May. William Bryant gave up his personal management of the affairs of Bryant & James at Plymouth and moved into London. The old partnership between him and May was revised. The new capital was to be an aggregate of the sums standing to the credit of the two partners at the time and, if larger sums were needed, they were to be provided equally. The new agreement also contained a clause that allowed each of the partners to introduce as an additional partner one of his sons 'who shall be 21'. This clause was to have far-reaching effects on the relationship between the two men, for May's sons were already following their own careers, whilst Bryant's sons* (all, like their father, forceful and determined personalities) were taken into the business, creating thus a rather formidable faction of Bryants against the kindly, mild-mannered May. The first step towards Bryant dominance was taken in 1863 when Wilberforce went into partnership and made factory manager at a salary of £300 a year.

Match Making at Bow: 1861–63

When production got under way at Fairfield Works, Bryant & May were at last able to supply the long-prepared British demand for safeties, and that the firm had not underestimated that demand was shown by its size. By the end of the first year the factory had reached a weekly output of over 1.8 million matches. One of the reasons for this immediate success was the fact that Bryant & May already had a first-class reputation for quality in the industry to which was added the sole rights for the manufacture in the United Kingdom of the new match that, apart from its obvious advantages, had a novelty value. The press campaign, so carefully planned in 1850, was at last initiated and was a great success. Fire insurance companies gave an enthusiastic welcome to safeties — one sending out a circular urging the use of 'only Bryant & May matches instead of lucifers which have caused immense loss of property and life'.

Another element in the success of the new enterprise was that Bryant & May's approach to match making was on a big-business scale, far more ambitious than that of most of their rivals operating from small premises with primitive methods of manufacture. Bryant & May's factory and financial backing were substantial and production was based on the most modern methods.

The splints were first machine-cut to the length of two matches. These were taken by girls who placed them in a machine which arranged (or 'filled') them into 'dipping frames', each holding 3,900

*Wilberforce Bryant, born 1836, Arthur Charles (1841) and the twins, Frederick and Theodore Henry (1843).

splints to yield 7,800 matches. The frames were then immersed in paraffin to increase the flammability of the splints. Both ends of the splints were then dipped in the igniting composition and, still in their frames, taken to a room where they were dried by the skilful use of steam-heated pipes and stoves and power-driven fans.

The matches (as they then were) were 'racked out' of the frames and deposited in narrow wooden trays which were taken to girls ('cutters down') who hand-cut each splint into two matches and to packers who boxed them. The packers became highly skilled at this final operation, seizing the exact number of matches for filling a box, and they could dexterously change the 'count' in the event of being given a larger or smaller box to fill. Frame-fillers were paid 1s 0d per 100 frames; cutters down $2\frac{3}{4}$d ($1\frac{1}{4}$p) the 'duck', *ie* three gross of small boxes or $2\frac{1}{2}$ gross of large boxes. Packers received 1s 9d (8p) the 100 boxes wrapped up. Children of up to 14 were paid about 4s 0d (20p) a week.

As in most other factories of that time, a large proportion of the labour was done by children for, as the law then stood, it was permissible to employ anyone over the age of nine years for up to 10 hours a day, and there were little in the way of health and safety regulations.* But in 1862, just as Fairfield Works got into full production, the government of the day set up a Commission on the Employment of Children in Industry which sent inspectors all over the country to collect evidence on conditions prevailing in match factories large and small.

The report of the Commission records an enlightened and humane attitude of the management of Bryant & May to its workers when compared to the grim conditions existing in most other match factories. In one such factory the inspectors found a boy of 10 employed in phosphorus dipping for 10 hours a day, and in another the dipper was helped 'by a small boy of eight actually leaning over the dipping stone'. At Bethnal Green, the inspectors found:

> a very small place employing about six men and fifteen boys. It consists of two small sheds, one a mere lean-to, the other like a cart hovel . . . with no ventilation whatever. This place serves for both dipping room and drying room as well as for mixing and heating the sulphur and phosphorus composition . . . The smell on entering this place is quite suffocating and one would think unendurable for any length of time. A white vapour may be seen constantly rising from the matches. Of course, places for washing *etc* could not be looked for here.

The white vapour, of course, was from the toxic white phosphorus. At King's Cross the inspectors visited the grandly-described Belle Isle Match Factory which they found to be 'a wretched place . . . much like a cow-house' and where they saw phosphorus matches stored in bulk near an open fire. They also found a number of children working in an ill-ventilated room

Frederick Bryant

Theodore Bryant

---

*The lower age-limit was ignored by the 'cottage industry' match makers.

Tower Hamlets Library

Mother and her children making match boxes at home at $2\frac{1}{2}d$ ($1\frac{1}{4}p$) a gross (144). This was better than the workhouse – but only just.

wherein phosphorus composition was mixed and a drying room 'close and hot from the stove where the mixture is heated':

> In the drying room the late owner . . . was burned to death a short time since trying to put out a fire. Outside at the back the arrangements are even worse. There is a water-butt with a little tub of sickly green water in it. Here, I was told, the children wash. Beyond this . . . is the yard . . . filled in the middle with a stagnant gutter. Here the children eat their meals, unless it be cold or wet, when they eat them round the stove. At the end of this yard, with an open sink or cesspool in front of it, is a single privy common to all, boys and girls alike, and in a very bad state. On one side of the yard was a little hay hovel in which a dog lived, but I could not make out that the children were allowed to eat their meals there. It would have been much better than the other places.

The children's wages in most of these small factories was 5d (2p) for a 10-hour shift and many of them were suffering with their teeth — a sure sign of phossy jaw in the match industry of those days.

The long section of the Commissioners' report dealing with Fairfield Works describes the healthy conditions prevailing there — which were a legacy of the Lundströms' Jönköping factory where, as it were, Bryant & May had learnt match making:

> These are spacious, airy works, with much open ground all round... They are in fact far removed from all other buildings... There is nothing unpleasant or objectionable here. The manufacture carried on here differs from that at other places insofar as no common phosphorus or other offensive ingredient is used.
>
> All the processes, with the exception of mixing the composition and drying the materials when dipped... are conducted in a long shed-like building, cut into compartments by wire caging. When a larger proportion of the building is ready, the boys will work in a part cut off from the girls by a party wall, and separate closets and washing places are being provided for each half... Along the walls are pegs, each with a number on it, on which the children and others hang their bonnets, coats, *etc*.
>
> Part of the manufacture consists in painting a composition, in appearance only much like the common composition, upon the sides of the match box. This is done by young women and girls, who are all provided with large strong leather aprons to protect their dresses. When a child has finished a frame or piece of work he takes it and receives a counter in exchange, and brings his counters at the end of the day in order to prevent any mistake in payment.
>
> Altogether this seems a very nicely conducted place. The children appear very happy and contented, and seem without exception much to prefer their employment here to that in other lucifer manufactories, in which most of them seem to have been engaged before. They give various reasons, mostly that this work is 'not so nasty', 'has no steam', or that they can earn more or are better treated here. Just as I arrived, 1 o'clock, a bell rang, and the children rushed out as if from school.

In an interview with the inspector William Bryant emphasised that the manufacture of safeties was

> ... perfectly free from any injurious influences upon the health of those engaged in it. We do not use the white phosphorus or common phosphorus at all. The only phosphorus used is not in the match, but applied to the outside of the box, on which the match is rubbed, and this phosphorus is of the red or amorphous kind, which is I believe perfectly harmless, and is not a poison.

When Francis May was interviewed he showed characteristically considerable interest in the education of the child workers — two hours a day of which was required by law. But, in contrast to Bryant, he admitted the existence of some degree of danger to health involved in the use of phosphorus:

> It is my experience... that the best educated workpeople are likewise the most efficient, the most economical, and the most respectful and attentive servants. But besides this, there is the very great advantage in a sanitary point of view in the system of schooling enforced on young children in this manufacture in particular. The supply of fresh air, which the interval of school time gives, does much to counteract the noxious vapours inhaled during the time of work. We receive here every year a report of the progress of the school. These reports are highly satisfactory, and we believe the school does a great deal of good.

When published in 1863, the report compared conditions at Fairfield Works favourably with all the other match factories dealt with and summed up by saying it was 'remarkable for the excellence of most of its arrangements, both for health and comfort of its workpeople'. This high standard set by the partners from the very beginning of their match-making enterprise was the result of an enlightened policy carried forward throughout the subsequent history of the firm.

The 1863 report also revealed some shocking facts concerning the 'cottage industry' of match-box making — already a major social scandal in Victorian England whereby nearly all match boxes were made through a system that used the sweated labour of slum women and their young children. The materials for the boxes consisted of wood-veneer and paper which were supplied by the factory and collected by the worker (who had to provide the paste); the price paid was usually about 2d (1p) per gross boxes. No training was required to go into this business and young children could make them. Match-box making was about the last resource of the destitute and the first occupation of little girls expected to earn some money between school hours. A dexterous child could earn 1d an hour and a hard-working woman up to 2d. At that rate, and putting in 12 hours a day, it was possible to make a living — provided enough work could be obtained.

Bryant and May relied almost wholly on importing machine-made match boxes from Sweden but in times of shortage had to turn to the homework system. For this they were in a position to pay marginally more than the standard rates prevailing. Then, in 1863, they purchased their own box-making machines from the Lundströms and installed them in a building especially designed for the purpose. In so doing the company took the first step in eliminating one of the more unpleasant aspects of 19th century *laissez-faire*, although at the time the move must have caused much suffering to some house-bound workers who preferred match-box making to the harsher alternative of the workhouse.

Museum of London

Mother and daughter making match boxes.

The First Ten Years 1861–71

The impact of Bryant & May's safety matches on the British market was such that the firm's imports of Swedish strike-anywhere matches fell from its record of 27,922,788 boxes in 1860 to 25,716,578 in the year when Fairfield Works started production. In 1862, Swedish imports were cut by half to 12,377,556 boxes. This drastic drop was not solely due to the advent of the safety match but mainly the result of foreign competition gaining ground. The problem was solved — probably for the first time, but certainly not the last — by the introduction of what is now called a 'fighting brand', *ie* matches of the usual quality but sold at a lower price and under a different label which did not indicate that they came from Sweden. In 1863, Bryant & May were able to order 21,594,924 boxes of strike-anywheres from Jönköping.

In the first few years after the opening of Fairfield Works the expansion in the volume and variety of matches produced was so rapid that between 1864 and 1868 the factory was in a continual state of enlargement. During the period several new varieties of matches were introduced including special damp-proof matches, safety cigar lighters, vesuvians, Congreve lights, a range of tapers and two types of wax-vestas. Also during this period Bryant & May started the manufacture of their own strike-anywhere phosphorus matches. At this time also, the company began producing a range of tin match boxes which became a profitable sideline to matches. The range included decorated match and taper holders and small metal pocket boxes for vesuvians and wax-vestas. The latter carried on the inside of the lids a selection of printed portraits of famous men and women of the day and, selling at one penny ($\frac{1}{2}$p), became

collectors' items rather like the cigarette cards which followed them.

Even though the company's main interest was centred on the Bow factory, the original business of general merchants was still continued at Whitechapel with the wholesaling of a bewildering range of goods which included Neave's baby food, Bovin's Real Old Windsor Soap, Oakey's knife-cleaning machines and Samson Barnett's diving apparatus. This side of the business was carried on by Francis May who had little to do with match making, which was managed by Bryant and his sons. Then, in 1868, May retired from the business altogether and devoted his energies to his farm at Reigate.

Three tin match boxes by Bryant & May and one by its subsidiary, Bell & Black.

OVERLEAF *A few of the many items from the Bryant & May range c1870.*

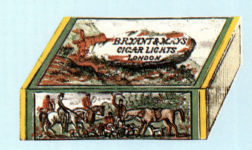

A block of 12 of the millions of excise stamps printed by the British Treasury in anticipation of the intended match tax.

Perhaps Francis May was not by temperament suited to the life and struggles of big business and maybe he was to some extent the loser of a battle with the five Bryants, for there is evidence that a serious rift occurred between him and William Bryant in the early years of Fairfield Works. A letter to May from a friend survives:

> I quite hope that all will end satisfactorily with W. B. Do not allow anything I may have said to interfere in any way with arranging with him as thou knows there are more than our idea of future increase of business floating in our minds and which must depend on circumstances whether they can be carried out or not. We can have another opportunity of talking over thou (*sic*) matters when we meet.

In two subsequent letters the same correspondent writes: 'I suppose W. B. is playing the waiting game, or cannot make up his mind to the best way to retrace his steps', and 'W. B. is playing his game cleverly, but he will find it hard to recover the advantage he has lost.'

The cause of the undoubted ill-feeling cannot now be known but it may be significant to the issue that on the departure of Francis May a new deed of partnership was drawn up between William Bryant and his four sons, in which the name of May does not appear. Thus the original small business of Francis May in Bishopsgate Without, which had become the largest maker and leading importer of matches in the United Kingdom was, in 1868, in all but name the Bryant family business. This was a takeover with a vengeance.

With the signature of the new partnership agreement, Wilberforce Bryant became the driving force of the firm: his policy was directed to more and more mechanisation linked with continual improvements in working conditions — an all too rare combination in those days.

The Match Tax Battle, 1871

In 1871 there occurred an event of historic interest in the British match industry. In his budget of April in that year* the Chancellor of the Exchequer, Robert Lowe, proposed a tax on matches of one halfpenny a box of 100 wooden matches and one penny a box of 100 vestas because, in the Chancellor's own words, the latter 'were more aristocratic'. It was estimated that the tax would yield £300,000 towards a budgetary deficit of £2.8 million.** This proposal was seen as a threat to the livelihood of thousands of match workers and resulted in a storm of protest both in parliament and in the East End of London where the major part of the British match industry was situated. The press also protested, and in a leading article on 24th April *The Times* declared:

> It is a tax upon a necessity of life; it is a tax on manufacture and upon one that gives remunerative employment to a great number of poor children . . .
> The duty which it is proposed to levy varies from 100 to 400 per cent on the wholesale price and the effect of this most extraordinary imposition will be almost entirely to extinguish two important branches of the business, throwing vast numbers of workpeople out of employment . . .
> Not only will the branches above referred to suffer but we are convinced that a great portion of the home trade will drift into the hands of foreigners as the demand will be for the lowest qualities which are principally manufactured abroad . . . Should the proposed tax become law the result to hundreds of families in the East End of London will be simply ruin.

Queen Victoria, who always took a keen interest in matters affecting her poorer subjects, was also moved to protest. Writing to the Prime Minister, Gladstone, she said:

> With respect to the Budget it is difficult not to feel considerable doubt as to the wisdom of the proposed tax on matches which is a direct tax and will be at once felt by all classes to whom matches have become a necessity of life.
> Their greatly increased price will in all probability make no difference in the consumption by the rich; but the poorer classes will be constantly irritated by this increased expense and reminded of the tax by the stamp on the box.
> Above all it seems certain that the tax will seriously affect the manufacture and sale of matches which is said to be the sole means of support for a vast number of the very poorest people and little children . . . so that this tax which is intended should press on all equally will in fact be only severely felt by the poor which would be very wrong and most impolitic at the present moment.

It was indeed a most impolitic moment, for there was then a revolutionary atmosphere in Europe which was alarming the British

*Which included an increase in the rate of income tax from £1 13s 4d (£1.67) to £2 4s 0d (£2.20) on £100.

**In the year ended 31st March 1984 the match tax provided £11.2 million for the government.

Cartoon comment on the outcome of the match-tax battle. (Will-o'-the Wisp, May 1871.)

'establishment'. On the very same day that the Queen wrote her letter, 3,000 match workers of London's East End (the majority being Bryant and May girls) gathered at a mass meeting in Victoria Park near Bow: there it was resolved that all those connected with the match industry should resist the tax by all possible legal means. It was further decided to carry a petition to the House of Commons on the following day.

Wheatley-Hubbard

The Chancellor match, introduced to celebrate the defeat of the match tax in 1871. The Exchequer match was designed for the same purpose but never issued. It bears a facsimile of a ½d postage stamp and an unflattering portrait of the then Chancellor, Robert Lowe.

OPPOSITE *The match tax victory. Public testimonial presented to Bryant & May.*

Accordingly the match workers gathered in Bow Road on the morning of Monday 24th April and formed an orderly procession led by women and children — many carrying banners with slogans. With remarkable discipline the procession marched as far as the Globe Bridge in Bow Road where it found a strong force of police waiting. Here the marchers obeyed an order to disperse but later reassembled at Mile End Gate. Again they were stopped by police, this time with some provocation, which resulted in scuffling and torn and broken banners.

Undeterred, the marchers assembled once more at Whitechapel Church where, in anticipation of further harassment from the police, they divided into small groups to make their ways as best they could to the Embankment near Blackfriars. Some covered the distance on foot, others went by river steamer, cart or wagon. By two o'clock in the afternoon the procession had re-formed at Blackfriars and the march to Westminster begun with a band playing and tattered banners flapping forlornly in the breeze. On arriving at the Houses of Parliament the match workers stood around Westminster Bridge whilst a small deputation went into Westminster Hall to present the petition. At that moment a large force of police rushed upon the waiting marchers and snatched

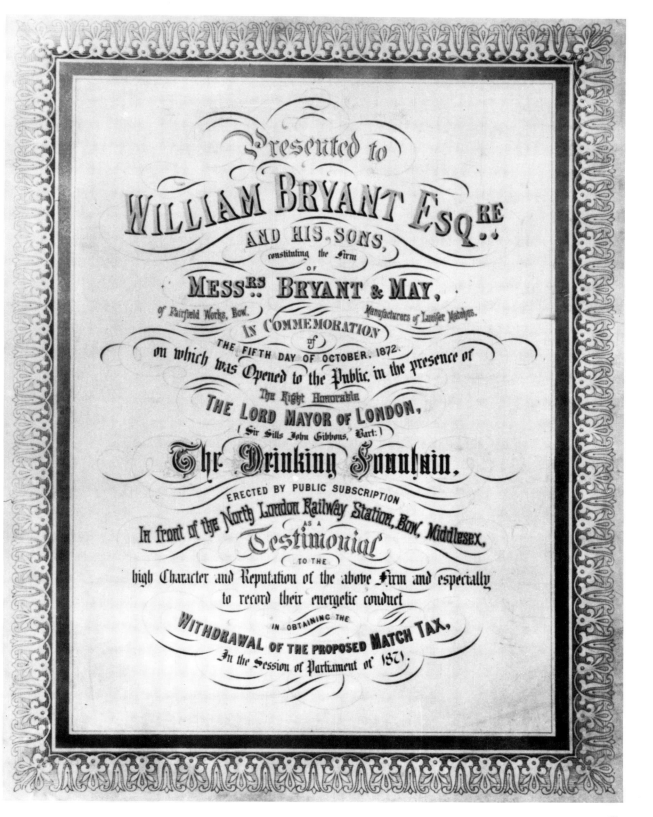

Opening of the Bryant & May drinking fountain at Bow on 5th October 1872. It remained there for 81 years.

away their banners which they threw into the Thames. Almost before the match workers knew what was happening their peaceful demonstration turned into a riot; stones were thrown and police batons swung as battle was joined. All entrances to New Palace Yard were blocked and, to escape the fury of the mob, the Chancellor of the Exchequer had to enter the House of Commons by an underground passage.

Gladstone, protected by a police escort and followed by jeers and boos, managed to get through. For several hours the battle continued until the demonstrators, exhausted after a day of marching and fighting, made their separate ways back to their homes.

A subsequent enquiry revealed that the violence was largely due to a number of political agitators who had deliberately used the march to create a disturbance. Indeed, it was the fear of such political elements that had impelled the police to use violent action against a peaceful march, for there was at the time in France a civil war between the Commune and the legal government. Gladstone's Liberal government was especially anxious to prevent any popular demonstration in England and the police had been instructed to react forcibly against processions or meetings of any political nature. Thus, the match workers became the bewildered victims of political events of which they knew nothing.

As a result, the violent and somewhat bloody end of that peacefully-intended demonstration brought immediate benefits to the match workers, for on the following day there were protests in parliament against the match tax and the brutality which had been used against people who only wanted to present a petition. Feelings on both sides of the house were so incensed that Robert Lowe, after consulting with Gladstone, announced:

> Notwithstanding the divisions that have occurred . . . Her Majesty's government have observed with regret that the proposition made by the government for placing a tax on matches has excited considerable dissatisfaction and disapprobation in many quarters . . . I have, therefore, announced that the measure with regard to matches will not be proceeded with.

Fitzroy Collection

A 'genuine' match-tax stamp LEFT *and a facsimile printed by Bryant & May for affixing to match boxes. For many years the slight difference convinced philumenists that the latter was a forgery.*

That night there was much rejoicing in the public houses of Bow and Bethnal Green. Later in the week a comic advertisement appeared in *Punch* magazine which read:

> To waste-paper dealers; to be disposed of; an immense quantity of unmatched classical literature, the writer having no further use for it and the authorities of the House compelling immediate clearance. Tenders to be sent to L. L. Brimstone, Budget Office, Somerset House. NB. This is an opportunity that will never occur again, as Mr. L. L. has resolved in future to get his tax first and consult the classics afterwards.

This witty skit referred to the millions of excise stamps already printed in anticipation of the match tax becoming law; each bore the Latin pun *Ex luce lucellum* (Out of light a little profit). In celebration of the defeat of the tax, Bryant & May produced a new brand of match called *Chancellor*. On the box was a facsimile of the stamp which Chancellor Lowe had so unwisely produced for the tax. The motto *Ex luce lucellum* could well have been permanently retained by Bryant & May.

By organising the leaders of the British match industry and by a campaign of lobbying members of parliament, Bryant & May had played a leading part in the defeat of the match tax and in 1872 the company was rewarded for its efforts by a public testimonial from subscriptions of a large number of people concerned with the trade and industry of Bow. This was a drinking fountain erected in the main street of Bow and it stood as a commemoration of the battle of the match tax until 1953.

Steady Growth 1872–83

The Bryant & May trademark of *Noah's Ark* was registered in January 1872. As a young man, William Bryant attended services at a Wesleyan chapel standing near to a public house called the 'Noah's Ark' and this is probably why the Ark, as a symbol of safety and security, struck him when he was later looking for a trade mark. But whatever its origin, this mark became famous and remains so today.

The following year brought about an important change in the firm's affairs, when it was decided to give up the Whitechapel warehouse and office and, together with these, the general merchandising side of the business, in order to concentrate entirely on match manufacture. In consequence a start was made to expand Fairfield Works.

Perhaps the decision to concentrate on match production was forced through the ill-health of William Bryant, for on 24th July 1874, he died suddenly at Eastbourne at the age of 70. Little is known of Bryant's private and business life but the rapid growth of the match business is evidence enough that he was a man of extraordinary business ability and foresight. He was succeeded as senior partner by his eldest son, Wilberforce.

The business which the four Bryant brothers inherited was already on its way to becoming the leader of the match industry of Great Britain. Its products were famous for their quality and had won medals at exhibitions all over Europe; within a few years they were to have similar successes in the United States and Australia.

It was realised by Wilberforce Bryant that more and better machinery was needed to produce matches of the existing high quality at a cost which would compete with the products of cheap continental labour. Foreign matches then had 20 per cent of the British market. In consequence many thousands of pounds were spent in experimenting with new machines and improving existing ones, and within a few years Fairfield Works was equipped with nearly 300 machines, each capable of automatically fitting 6,000 splints at a time into the dipping frames. In addition there was other labour-saving machinery. Power was supplied by 25 steam engines of 500 hp each driving overhead shafting.

This re-equipment of the factory enabled Bryant & May to reach a daily output of 1.728 million boxes of wooden matches (selling retail at 7½d (3p) a dozen boxes), 500,000 boxes of wax-vestas and many thousands of boxes of vesuvians and other lights. To sell this considerable output against severe competition, the firm initiated a vigorous publicity campaign through advertising in the press, on public transport in the big cities and through the publication of a diary and almanac which had a wide circulation.

By the time Wilberforce took over from his father, the firm had a splint-making mill at Bow Common. Here, every year thousands of tons of yellow Canadian pine were converted into splints.

Set in the overall pattern of the industrial conditions of that

The first match box to bear the famous Bryant & May trade mark (1872).

Production unit at Fairfield Works in the 1870s. In all industries at that time the 'bowler' was a 'status symbol' which marked the wearer as a craftsman, foreman etc. The bare feet of the boy workers denote a different status.

Match-box making at Bow c1880. Bryant and May started mechanical box making in 1863 but employed hand workers during times of heavy demand.

Mass production at Fairfield Works. Women and boys with bowler-hatted foremen, working under gaslights in the 1890s.

Tin match boxes by Bell & Black.

time, Fairfield Works was a model of consideration for the welfare of its workers; for this was a period when the theory of *laissez-faire* was generally put into practice and labour was exploited to the limit. Conditions in London's East End were specially bad but by the standards prevailing the wages paid by Bryant & May were good. Working by the piece with modern machinery, women could earn up to 12s 0d (60p) a week — then a very good wage for a factory worker — and children were paid 'in proportion'. As the firm was by then producing strike-anywhere matches, particular attention was paid to cleanliness and ventilation and the factory had a visiting doctor and dentist to watch for any early signs of phosphorus necrosis among the workers.

The production of tinplate articles was also expanded during this period, mainly through the acquisition of the rights to a new process for printing on tin — a process which was a great advance on the old method of transfer. The necessary machinery was installed in the Reading works of Huntley, Bourne & Stevens,* tin-box makers to the biscuit firm of Huntley & Palmer, and production began in 1878. Bryant & May then launched an extensive press campaign to announce its new range of tinplate goods which they said (inaccurately) was produced from first to last — both printing and manufacturing — in their own works:

> Bryant & May having now perfected their new Patent Tin Printing processes, and having erected most complete machinery — taking advantage of all the very latest machinery — beg to draw attention to the following articles of daily use, which they can offer of the very best quality and designs at very low prices.
>
> By their very new printing process they can obtain results never hitherto attempted on metal, and can give a variety of detailed and complicated patterns and designs that add very materially to the appearance and value of the various articles produced.

These 'articles of daily use' included tea and coffee canisters, tobacco and snuff boxes, collar and glove boxes, trays and biscuit boxes. Over the following years the range of tinplate products increased to include hundreds of different items — pen, pencil, pin, trinket and cachou boxes; 'sanitary dredgers in decorated, crystallized or plain tin'; lozenge, spice, Seidlitz powder, palette and bonbon boxes; tins for blacking, polish and even artist's oil-colours. Most of these containers were sold packed with up to a dozen boxes of Bryant & May matches. As a vehicle for selling matches, the tinplate business was an advertising method which made a profit even though the items sold for only a few pence each.

Cheap though these artifacts were, they attracted the condescending attention of the *Royal Album of Arts and Industries*:

> Bryant & May do a large business in those pretty tea canisters, biscuit tins, and fancy tins of all kinds which one cannot help noticing in every grocer's window; many of these are made out of one piece of metal. The patterns are most artistic, indeed, they are almost too good for such low-priced articles.

*Huntley was known to Bryant and May through the Society of Friends.

If the canisters and boxes were scarce and high-priced, they would be valued more than they are. English people, unfortunately, seldom judge a thing from an artistic standpoint. The first question usually is, 'How much did it cost?' and, if the article is perfectly useless, and ugly into the bargain, it is highly valued if it cost a good round sum.

Many of the designs printed upon the tin boxes by Bryant & May's patent process are copied from rare works of art, and thus the poorest individual can adorn his cottage with articles which would, in the days of our grandfathers, have been deemed worthy of a place on the sideboards of the well-to-do.

In the early 1880s the firm turned its attention to the expansion of its already extensive export markets and particular efforts were made to enter the USA match market. In 1883 agreement was

The model Post Office pillar box filled with wax vestas.

LEFT ABOVE *The Bryant & May 'Very Ornamental Glove Box', with 12 boxes of matches, retailed at 1s 6d (7½p).*

LEFT *The Family Match Safe, 2s 6d (12½p), contained 36 boxes of matches and three ornamental match-box cases.*

LEFT *Metal taper boxes sized 6, 9 and 12 inches, each containing white or coloured wax tapers and retailing at from 6d (2½p) to 1s 0d (5p).*

RIGHT *Decorated metal boxes.*

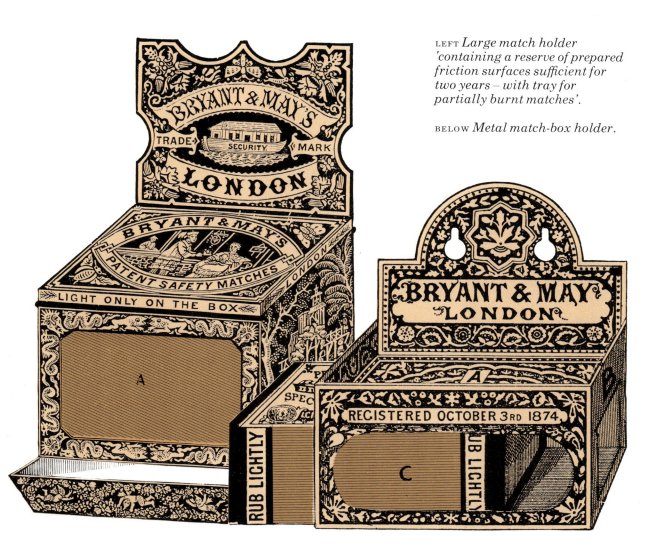

LEFT *Large match holder 'containing a reserve of prepared friction surfaces sufficient for two years – with tray for partially burnt matches'.*

BELOW *Metal match-box holder.*

Round wax-vesta holders in wood and metal.

reached with the Diamond Match Corporation of America for the sale of safety matches in the USA over a period of 10 years. But many difficulties, including tariff problems, were met with and the agreement was cancelled after only four years. On the other hand, exports to other parts of the world expanded steadily. A survey established that Bryant & May matches were by far the most popular in many countries — especially in China, despite the fact that the Chinese themselves were making matches and, moreover, exporting them to Britain. Few records concerning Bryant & May's exports at this time have survived but that they were very large is shown by the bewildering range of the firm's match-box labels for that particular period.

Bryant & May started in the match business as importers but by 1890 they were exporting all over the world.

Foreign customers all demanded their own designs on the boxes. Japanese and Chinese customers insisted on brightly coloured pictures as it was their habit to decorate room walls with match-box labels. India favoured tigers, while Australians preferred dryads sitting by gurgling brooks, or ships sailing for some distant port. There were likes and preferences in the United Kingdom too, especially for the colour of match heads. Miners in the north favoured black-tipped matches, Preston and Limerick demanded blue, Lancashire liked pink, and Ireland red.

With sales expanding both at home and overseas a stage had been reached which called for a completely new and important development in the company's affairs.

A Public Company 1884–87

Alongside the rapid expansion in the activities of the company under the leadership of Wilberforce Bryant there had been major changes in its internal structure, Arthur Bryant having died early in 1882 and Theodore having left the business later in the same year. Thus in 1884 the firm was being run by Wilberforce and Frederick Bryant alone. In these circumstances the two remaining brothers decided to convert Bryant & May into a public limited company. The reasons for this move were explained by Wilberforce at the first shareholders' meeting of the new company:

> Two years ago my youngest brother retired leaving only two brothers and myself to carry on the business. Then last May we lost another brother. In consequence we felt it unwise to carry on the business alone. We wished then to put the business on a permanent basis whilst we still had health and strength, so in the event of death or ill health it could be successfully carried on. This is our sole reason for converting and it is not without regret that we allow the business to pass even partially from our hands.

Bryant & May Limited was formed in June 1884 with a capital of £300,000, consisting of 60,000 preference shares of £5 which were quickly taken up. The following year there was a further issue of 20,000 preference shares of £5.

During the time of the formation of the company, the Bryant brothers were approached by two London match manufacturers, Pace & Sons and J S Hunt & Company, with the proposal that their two businesses might be absorbed by Bryant & May. This was agreed, although the factory of Pace & Sons continued to manufacture independently under the supervision of the parent company.

The board of Bryant & May Limited was under the chairmanship of Wilberforce Bryant who, with his brother Frederick as a director, and his cousin Henry Carkeet as secretary, ensured that the Bryant family still held a powerful position in the firm. The rest of the board consisted of men who were prominent in the match industry. Otto Trummer, the head of an important match exporting firm, was persuaded to give up his business and join Bryant & May. In addition, E C Pace of Pace & Sons and E M Dixon of the match-making firm, Bell & Black, were appointed to the board. Another Bell & Black staff member to join the firm was Gilbert Bartholomew — an appointment which brought great strength to the company, for he was a man of extraordinary ability who later became chairman of Bryant & May and a dominating figure in the British match industry.

In forming the company, Wilberforce Bryant was determined to make it into a co-operative concern: for many of its employees had grown up with Bryant & May and he considered it just that they should have a beneficial interest in a business which they had helped to develop. Shares were therefore allotted to all heads of departments — and to long-serving employees. The firm's travellers

Matches for use in motor cars, lifeboats and other windy places.

and some of its best customers were also offered shares which they took up. Net profit for the first six months of the company's life was £33,044.

The expansion on which Bryant & May were determined continued in 1885, when an approach was made by the London matchmaking firm of Bell & Black Limited offering itself for sale. This company was established at Bow in 1839 to make matches, vestas, tapers and metal boxes. In 1881 it amalgamated with three other match manufacturers with factories in Manchester, Glasgow and York and became a public company with an issued capital of £250,000. From that time business steadily declined to the extent that Bryant & May were able to purchase Bell & Black's four factories, plant, stock and goodwill for £54,490. Bell & Black continued to make matches under their own name until 1888.

Bryant & May were now in a strong position to meet the challenge which faced British match makers, for while the demand for matches continued to increase, the pressure from foreign competition grew with it.

Since it was not possible in that heyday of free trade to persuade the government to protect the home industry, it was left to Bryant & May to compete with cheap foreign matches through efficient production, good quality and aggressive salesmanship. To accomplish this aim, further improvements were made in machinery to simplify and increase production and further to improve the quality of the products. By 1888 every department was to some extent mechanised — box making, in particular, which was entirely automated.

The mechanisation programme was linked to a new drive for export markets. Sales to Australia rose steadily and by 1888 Bryant & May matches were selling in Melbourne alone at the rate of 1,000 cases a month. Sales to New Zealand also increased.

Much of the success in the export market was due to Frederick Bryant. It was he who penetrated India and a number of other Far Eastern countries, where the demand for matches was becoming firmly established.

In 1885 Francis May died at his Reigate home at the age of 83. There can be little doubt that the contrasting, yet complementary, characters of Francis May and William Bryant had much to do with their early success, for in the days when the firm's various activities were conducted on a personal basis, much must have depended on May's kindly and friendly nature which so strongly contrasted with Bryant's down-to-earth, yet intuitive, attitudes. Again, there can be no doubt that the Bryant family's benevolent relationship with the Bow workers was largely inspired by Francis May.

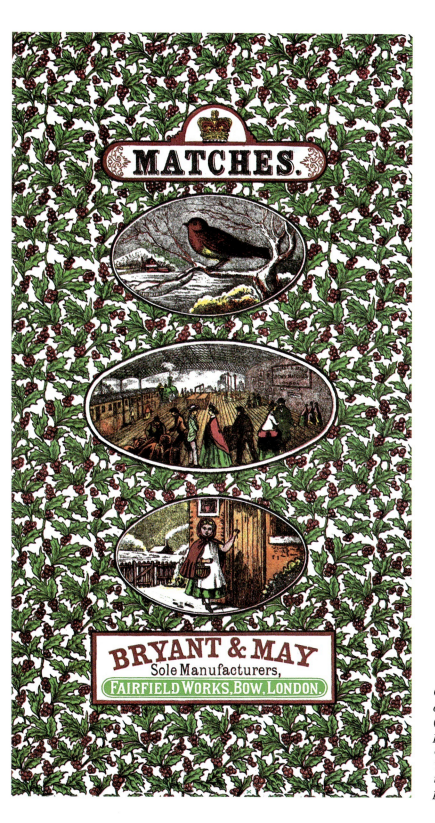

Christmas wrapping for one dozen boxes of Portrait matches (1873). It features the growing popularity of Christmas travel brought about by the railways. Then, as now, the company used topical subjects to sell its products.

The Matchgirls' Strike 1888

In 1888 the company was involved in an event which is part of the history of the British working-class movement, and which produced the first women's trade union, the Union of Women Match Makers. The 1880s was a decade of serious industrial unrest in Britain, and 1888 saw many long and bitter trade disputes, including strikes by coalminers, engineers, dock workers and seamen. In July there occurred a strike of the Bryant & May matchgirls.

The complex issues behind the strike at Fairfield were exploited by the Fabian reformer, Annie Besant, the journalists Leigh Hunt and W T Stead, and Sidney Webb the social reformer. In theory the dispute was over low wages — but only in theory, for the average potential wage at Fairfield Works was 11s 2d (56p) a week which, for a factory worker, was a very good wage indeed. However, as this was earned by piece work, what the matchgirls actually received depended largely on their own industry, and in this they were well known to be erratic. They stayed away from the factory when they felt like it and often only a small proportion of the workforce turned up on a Monday morning or on a day when anything of interest was occurring elsewhere.

This situation was confirmed by the social investigator, Charles Booth, in his survey, *Life and Labour in London*. He remarks of the matchgirls that 'irregularity of attendance reduced the girls' earnings and so made the wages appear lower than they were'. But there was another, seasonal, factor that affected wages in the match industry. This was the considerable fall in the demand for matches during the summer months. This slack period was usually compensated for by the extra call for women workers in the jam factories and, to a great extent, by the fact that many matchgirls liked to go hop- and fruit-picking in the summer. Thus, those that remained at match making were able to work full shifts. However, the hop- and fruit-picking season of 1888 was singularly bad and few women could find work on farms or in factories. Bryant & May's response to this situation was to share out the amount of available work rather than resort to laying off workers. It then followed that wages were reduced and some hardship resulted. This was the main cause for the strike of the matchgirls.

The situation at Fairfield Works was eagerly seized upon by the Fabian Society which, on 23rd June, published in its journal *The Link*, an article entitled *White Slavery in London*. This stated that while holders of Bryant & May shares were receiving a dividend of 20 per cent, the matchgirls at Fairfield Works were being paid only four shillings a week and that 'even this pittance was subjected to all manner of deductions and fines'.

The article went on to say that the girls were ill-treated by foremen; that girls had been brought in from Scotland so as to reduce wages paid to the London workers; that the company was buying up other match-making firms to form a monopoly and further reduce wages, and that all workers had a shilling a week

Tower Hamlets Library

The 1888 strike committee. Standing (in light-coloured dress) is Annie Besant, celebrated 'theosophist' and champion of women's rights: next to her, Herbert Burrows, reformer of factory conditions. The others are Bryant & May matchgirls.

To help combat the evils of the cottage match-making industry, and what it considered to be unsatisfactory conditions at the Fairfield Works, the Salvation Army operated its own match factory at Lamprell Street, Bow. The Army supported the matchgirls' strike by donating 5s 0d (25p) to the strike fund.

Label especially designed and printed for a customer. Bryant & May were among the first to use the match-box label as an advertising medium.

deducted to pay for a statue of Gladstone which Theodore Bryant had erected in Bow Road. The fact that most of these charges were without foundation was shown by a subsequent enquiry made by the London Trades Council.

But accurate or not, the article started a campaign of calumny and abuse directed against the directors and shareholders of Bryant & May. There were more articles in *The Link*, and other radical journals joined the campaign. All the articles on the subject were written in sensational, dramatic terms often bordering on the hysterical. They are typified by one such piece in *The Link* which had more concern with the rate of dividends paid to shareholders than with wages and conditions at Fairfield Works:

> The public attention lately drawn to the infamous conditions under which the girls worked who earned for the idle shareholders of the Bryant & May Company Limited their enormous dividends, has raised the whole question of Ethics of Shareholding.
>
> Hitherto, men and women have sought a 'good investment' and have winked at the injustice and the oppression which were implied in the 'goodness' of the investment. Country clergymen, venerated ecclesiastics of high rank, decent men of business who, on every Sunday, in church or chapel, thanked God that they were not as other men, and as dividend day came round slipped their unearned wealth into their pockets, unheeding how that wealth was made, at what price it was earned — all these have been startled from their smug complacency and many are uneasily asking, 'What can I do to rid myself of blood-guiltiness?'
>
> One clergyman wrote to us, stating that he had sold his shares. But to what avail this hasty shifting of responsibility? If every shareholder whose conscience is aroused is to get rid of his shares, the control of the company will fall into harsher hands and the conditions of the workers will be worsened . . .
>
> To sell shares is to throw paper into hands that may be unscrupulous. Let humane and honest shareholders keep their shares, pay over their dividends to the Union of Women Match Makers, press on the directors changes for the benefit of the workers, and attend the next meeting to force improvements on the company . . . Would that some easy-going shareholders would come through some alleys in Bethnal-Green and Shoreditch, and see the sources of their wealth. Never again would they dare to spend, save in human service, the exhaustion, the shame, of the white slaves who toil and die that they may live in loathsome and scandalous sloth.

This extraordinary outpouring accompanied a well-organised campaign by which members of parliament were circularised, posters exhibited and demonstrations held in Hyde Park. On one occasion a giant match box was paraded carrying the words 'Thirty-eight per cent dividend' and containing the figure of a clergyman praying for higher dividends.

Thus were the disgruntled matchgirls at Fairfield Road further incited and when, on 5th July, two of them were dismissed for insubordination, a spark was set to the powder keg. The matchgirls had always shown a remarkable power of combination — particularly those of Fairfield Works who all lived near one another in Bow and the surrounding area. They were distinguished by a strong *esprit de corps*, any one girl's grievance being adopted by all the others. Therefore on the dismissal of the two girls there was general discontent in the factory.

The directors at once compromised by withdrawing the dismissal notices, but matters had gone too far. Some 1,000 girls left work there and then and the factory was closed. One hundred strikers marched to Fleet Street and sent a deputation to see Mrs Besant who, with her fellow reformers, immediately took up the cause of the strike. Committees were organised and funds raised from which, during the two weeks of the dispute, 700 girls received strike pay of four to five shillings a week. George Bernard Shaw was one of the cashiers.

The strike became a national issue with the press of left and right ranged against each other. *The Link* continued its lurid tales of the horrors of the conditions at Bryant & May's factory whilst *The Times* took up the other side in a number of leading articles and a score of readers' letters. On 14th July the editor of *The Times* rejoiced:

> The strike of the matchgirls ... is still going on ... It is not possible that this state of things can go on indefinitely. Their most ardent sympathisers will not be willing to continue to support them in voluntary or enforced idleness. They must either return to their old work or must find new work of another kind, thereby reducing by their competition the miserably poor wages of unskilled female labour in the East End of London.
>
> It is a dismal prospect, but such as this is almost certainly the end of a strike entered upon with inadequate resources and at the instigation of agitators who make it the business of their lives to sow discord between employers and employed ... The pity is that the matchgirls have not been suffered to take their own course, but have been egged on to strike by irresponsible advisers. No effort has been spared by those pests of the modern industrial world, the Social Democrats, to bring the quarrel to a head. Messrs Bryant & May have been picked out by the agitators for special obloquy and attack.

The strike ended on 21st July following a meeting between Bryant & May directors and representatives of the London Trades Council (a labour organisation). The matchgirls returned to work with a number of concessions. It was agreed that the system of fines should be abolished and, instead, insubordination should be punished by dismissal; no striker would be penalised; the Union of Women Match Makers would be recognised by the management for the settlement of the workers' grievances; small deductions from the box-makers' wages to cover paste and brushes were also abolished. There were a number of other concessions.

After the settlement, the London Trades Council issued a report on the entire affair in which it was actually shown that most of the charges levelled against the company were without foundation. It was established that in normal times workers in Bryant & May were paid from 15 to 20 per cent more than similar labour in other industries; that women were earning from 12 to 14 shillings a week and some considerably more. The charge that a shilling had been deducted from wages to pay for the statue of Gladstone was com-

Emptying match coils c 1890. Match splints in the length of two matches were rolled into coils and dipped at both ends. They were then taken off and passed on for cutting into halves.

pletely false and the vast amount in fines said to have been imposed on the workers dwindled on investigation to a total sum of eight pounds over a period of three months; it was also shown that the policy of mechanisation had increased the girls' earning capacity.

The strike of the matchgirls resulted in a whetting of public interest in the match industry and, when peace was restored, journalists from many of the leading newspapers arrived at Fairfield Works hoping later to write about the appalling conditions described in *The Link*. Most of them were surprised at what they found. Writing in *The Record* of 19th October, one correspondent described how he:

> ... went to the works with a vivid recollection of the sensational reports that appeared in certain periodicals a short time since as to the oppressed conditions of the workers. The dividends of shareholders, it was said, were gained at the cost of 'starvation, the exhaustion, the shame of white slaves, who toil and die that they (the shareholders) may live in loathsome and scandalous sloth.' I was, therefore, not a little surprised to find, instead of a row of ramshackle sheds, a stately building worthy of the best traditions of English labour. But there were other surprises in store.
>
> On a closer acquaintance with the interior of the workrooms, it was apparent that every provision had been made for the comfort and convenience of the workers. Each department was so well ventilated that the fumes from the sulphur and other concoctions used in the manufacture of the goods were hardly noticeable, even to a stranger.
>
> The various rooms were warm, dry and clean, and seats were provided wherever it was possible for the workers to take advantage of them. So far as regards the match makers themselves, one looked in vain for even a single individual whose appearance would at all support the description of them above noticed.
>
> I saw in all more than a thousand hands, and they were without doubt some of the most light-hearted workers I have ever come across. The great majority of them were girls or young women, but, so far from being 'slaves', they apparently enjoyed far more freedom than many a domestic. They were well clad, although it must be admitted that in many instances the attire was more gaudy than neat; but then, what is an East End factory girl if she is not arrayed in all the colours of the rainbow?
>
> There were no traces of starvation; most of the girls seemed to be remarkably well nurtured and many of them had bright rosy cheeks which contrasted pleasantly with the pale and sickly countenances of many mill-hands in Lancashire. Not one of them showed the least sign of weariness or exhaustion; on the contrary in nearly every room the girls were working away with all their will and the merry ditties or choruses that some of them were singing and others whistling scarcely indicated depressed spirits.
>
> There was, of course, strict discipline in every department, but it is evident that the foremen are esteemed as well as obeyed by the hands ... The mutual goodwill between the overseers and workers explains much of the harmony that existed at Fairfield Works in the past and augurs well for the future.

Most of the other journalists who visited the factory wrote similar reports and it was on this note that the saga of the matchgirls' strike ended.

Important Developments 1888–1901

One of the concessions made to the strikers was the provision of a separate dining room for the women workers and from this developed the opening of a girls' club opposite the main gates of Fairfield Works. This provided comfortable accommodation where the girls could have a good, cheap meal and a room was set aside for relaxation and reading. Soon after its inauguration the club was serving up to 60,000 meals a year at a cost of 3d each. From the time of its opening the firm's directors encouraged the club and supported it financially. A quarter of a century later it became the Gilbert Bartholomew Memorial Girls' Club, almost entirely financed by the company, and was one of the first industrial welfare institutions.

It was during the year of the strike that Frederick Bryant retired from the company to be replaced on the board by Gilbert Bartholomew who had been general manager since 1885. In due course Bartholomew became chairman and an outstanding figure in the firm's history.

In 1891 output at Fairfield Works reached a new record with the production of 360 million boxes of 100 strike-anywhere matches, 52 million boxes of safeties, 23 million vesuvians and 105 million wax-vestas. By this time a good export trade had been built up in America and the firm's New York agent was offering a variety of 62 items of various matches in different boxes. This high level of production was achieved in the face of still increasing foreign competition by reducing the cost of production whilst still maintaining a high standard of quality.

Towards the end of the century there were two important developments which affected the match industry in general and Bryant & May in particular. One was the advent of the continuous process match-making machine, the other the discovery of a non-poisonous substance to replace yellow phosphorus (also known as white phosphorus).

Although the invention of the safety match had lessened the danger of phossy jaw in match making, the main demand was still for the strike-anywhere match which included poisonous yellow phosphorus in the head, and Bryant & May were making some 36,000 million of these a year. Although widespread and stringent precautions against phosphorus necrosis were taken at Fairfield Works this scourge was not entirely absent among the workers.

In 1893 a Royal Commission on Labour published *A Report on Phosphorus Poisoning* based on evidence it had collected from the British match industry. The report makes horrifying reading and shows that conditions in many match factories were no better than they were in the days of the 1862 investigation. One male worker who had been employed as a dipper for many years and who had, miraculously one might think, escaped phossy jaw, told the Commission of the many people he had known to die of the disease and of some 20 who had 'lost their jaw'. Of one he said, 'You could take his chin (demonstrating) and shove it all into his mouth.' He had seen another dipper 'with his hand all plastered with the stuff [phosphorus] eating his bread and butter, and taking it all in together'. This man lost his jaw after two years.

A different story emerged from the inspection of Fairfield Works. Even Tom Mann, trade unionist and Communist, had nothing but praise for the measures taken at Bryant & May's to combat the disease. In a letter appended to the Commission's Report he expressed 'complete satisfaction' at finding that the dipping rooms were isolated with no workers above them, whereas (he said) he had supposed that the fumes from the dipping rooms circulated throughout the factory.

Five years later the factory was again inspected, this time by a deputation from the London United Workmen's Committee who reported that they were:

> both surprised and pleased at the precautions taken to prevent . . . necrosis, and found that every requirement of the Factory Acts and special rules had been more than fully complied with, as well as everything that had been suggested from outside, which was calculated to conduce to the welfare of the workers.
>
> The deputation found upon making careful enquiries that notwithstanding the glaring and misleading statements made by certain sections of the press, that during the last 20 years only 47 cases of necrosis have occurred at these works, and 81 per cent of those attacks have been completely cured, and many of those attacked are still in the factory in the enjoyment of full health, and as the company pay their wages to those on the sick list, it is not likely to lessen the same.

The militant feminist, Millicent Garrett Fawcett, also visited Fairfield Works in 1893 and wrote in the London *Standard*, 23rd July:

> . . . it would take too long to narrate in detail all that we saw of the precautions that are used with the view of preventing necrosis . . . the whole factory was splendidly ventilated, and the girls and women employed had a rosy, healthy look of those who habitually live in the open air . . .
>
> The firm makes exceptionally liberal allowances to their employees if they are absent from sickness — whether from necrosis or any other cause . . . one worker receiving 10 shillings a week for three years: and other cases are given 20 shillings or 25 shillings a week or even more.

But nevertheless, as these reports indicated, Fairfield Works was not entirely free from the dreadful disease of phossy jaw. But the cases that did occur were usually the fault of the sufferer. The main cause of phosphorus necrosis was the penetration of the fumes of yellow phosphorus into the jaw bone through cavities in decayed teeth and the only way to prevent this was a management policy of ensuring that workers maintained complete dental health by regular inspection and, if necessary, treatment by the company's own dentist. But, as the 1893 Report pointed out, the workforce at Bryant & May:

Fire drill at Fairfield Works c1900.

hated to have their teeth seen to, and thought it was quite a good joke to take the doctor in and make him believe their teeth were sound when they were not . . . They believed that there was no fear of necrosis if they washed their hands before eating and that therefore 'If yer want to have it, you can have it; it's yer own fault.'

An example of the dreadful results of this attitude occurred at Fairfield Works at about this time when a man, employed in the dipping room for 20 years with the best of health, went out during his dinner hour and had a tooth drawn by a dentist not employed by the firm. He went straight back to work and contracted severe necrosis.

To prevent even isolated cases of the disease, the company commissioned a Mr H H Drake to produce ideas to combat it. Amongst drawings he submitted was one of match-box fillers working with their hands thrust through tight-fitting sleeves into a glass case which was intended to confine the fumes.* Another drawing showed dippers working with their heads enclosed in grotesque masks with glazed sight holes in front and a high 'chimney' on top. Although ingenious, these inventions were clumsy and unlikely to be popular with the workers. They were never used.

The answer to the problem of phossy jaw came in 1898 when two French chemists, Sevène and Cahen, discovered that the non-poisonous sesquisulphide of phosphorus could be used to make the strike-anywhere match instead of yellow (or 'white') phosphorus. This marked the beginning of the end of phossy jaw.

In 1900, Bryant & May acquired the British patent rights in the safe phosphorus and after a period of development substituted it for the poisonous yellow variety. In 1908, the company offered its licence rights free to all United Kingdom match makers on the condition that the government put an absolute prohibition on the use of yellow phosphorus. This was agreed and in 1910 the White Phosphorus (Matches Prohibition) Act came into effect, banning both manufacture and import of yellow phosphorus matches. Phossy jaw was thereby eliminated in Britain and, within a short time, the rest of the match-making world.

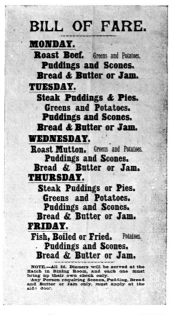

Canteen menu c1900.

---

*Possibly a Bryant & May 'first', and if so, a remarkable example of technological forecasting, for similar devices are used today in the handling of dangerous materials.

Match workers leaving Fairfield Works for the lunch break.

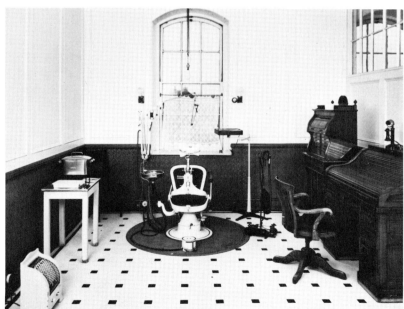

The most effectual weapon against the scourge of 'phossy jaw' was regular dental examination and treatment. Fairfield Works had its own dentist and dental surgery.

Diamond Match Company 1901

The invention and introduction of a single machine to carry out all the processes of match making was the most important technical development in the history of the match industry. It is difficult to exaggerate the advantages brought about by the invention. The process wrought so great a change in manufacturing operations, both in the conditions under which they were performed and in the rate of output, that to describe the machine is to describe a new industry.

The continuous process machine appeared in Sweden in 1864 and was first mass-produced by the Diamond Match Company of America. The Diamond machine could, in a consecutive series of movements, cut match splints from blocks of seasoned pine, insert them in holes in connected metal plates (known as a 'match-chain'), dip them in paraffin, then in the striking composition. One machine was capable of making 576,000 matches in an hour.

Encouraged by the success of the machine in the USA, Diamond Match sold it to match manufacturers in France and Germany but could find no purchasers in the United Kingdom. The reasons why Bryant & May refused the machine are not known but it is possible that the asking price was too high or that Bryant & May were not convinced by the performance claims of the makers. Whatever the reasons, the decision was to have far-reaching consequences for the company.

Being unable to exploit their machine in the United Kingdom, Diamond Match decided to make matches in Britain themselves and, in 1895, took over the small Bootle match business of Collard, Kendall & Company, demolished that firm's works and erected on its site a large factory which was then considered to be the finest of its kind in the world. It was equipped with 16 of the new 'cut, set and dip' machines and was thus capable of producing some 92 million matches in a day.* In 1896 the factory went into the production of three well known brands of matches acquired from Collard, Kendall & Company. These were *Captain Webb*, first produced in 1876, *Puck*, produced in 1888 and *Swan Vestas*, introduced in 1883 and already on the way to becoming one of the most famous brands in the world.

Almost immediately after the opening of the Bootle factory, Bryant & May began to feel the effects of competition from the up to date manufacturing process that enabled Diamond to sell *Captain Webb* and *Puck* matches at 1s 0d (5p) per gross of boxes as against Bryant & May's *Pearl* and *Tiger* matches at 1s 8d (8½p) per gross, and *Ruby* at 1s 7d per gross. This competition made particularly heavy inroads into Bryant & May's business in the north of England.

The new rival had appeared at a most unfortunate time, for the

TOP *Collard, Kendall & Company's original design for the Captain Webb label c1876 and* ABOVE *as re-designed by Bryant & May.*

---

*One brand of which was known as *The Drunkard's Match*. The splints of these were treated chemically so that they would not burn beyond midpoint.

firm was experiencing other difficulties with plummeting sales in Australia and a deterioration in home sales through the old enemy of cheap foreign imports. It was under these conditions that the directors of Bryant & May began to consider a merger with the British Diamond Match Company.

The idea of an amalgamation had been considered by both companies for some years and never acted upon. But with the conditions existing in 1901, it was apparent to both sides that continued competition between the two powerful enterprises, each enjoying certain advantages over the other, would have serious consequences to the prosperity of both. A merger on the other hand offered mutual benefits.

Agreement between the two companies was reached in June 1901 whereby Bryant & May purchased the goodwill, assets and rights of the British Diamond Match Company for £480,000 and the American company acquired 54.5 per cent of the share capital of Bryant & May. The purchased assets included the Bootle factory, Diamond's interests in two South African match factories at Port Elizabeth and Cape Town, 75,000 acres of pine forest in California and whole ownership of the Irish Match Company. There was also agreement concerning foreign markets whereby the American company undertook not to manufacture or sell matches in any part of the British Commonwealth outside the West Indies, whilst Bryant & May agreed not to manufacture in North America or the West Indies.

On the face of it, this agreement seems to have been a 'reverse takeover' but during the years 1914–18 the American shares were gradually purchased by investors in the United Kingdom and control passed out of American hands. Following the merger, the board of Bryant & May was re-formed to include four ex-Diamond directors with Wilberforce Bryant as chairman.

The benefits arising from the merger were almost immediate, for Bryant & May's profits, which for some years had been dwindling, rose within a year by 100 per cent. This was mainly because the continuous process machinery at the Bootle factory enabled the company to produce high-grade matches which could compete with cheap imports. Similar machines were installed at Fairfield Works in 1904.

In the long view the most important outcome of the merger was the association in management of Gilbert Bartholomew and George Paton, one of the Diamond directors who had joined the board of Bryant & May. These two men, one English with a quarter of a century of experience in the match trade, the other a Scotsman with wide business training, were mainly responsible for changing the entire outlook of the company and leading it into the changing world of the 20th century.

More labels c1900.

Printing labels at Fairfield Works, Bow c1905.

PART TWO

By building up its own large fleet of steam lorries, Bryant & May were in the forefront of the shift from rail to road transport.

YEARS OF GROWTH

Modernisation and Expansion 1902–14

By 1902 Bryant & May were the biggest and most successful match manufacturers in Britain and still one of the largest importers of Swedish matches — a connection which lasted until the agency was disposed of in 1910. Under the management of Gilbert Bartholomew and George Paton, the company spread its activities to other parts of the world. South Africa became the first objective when, in 1904, Bartholomew visited that country.

Through the amalgamation with the Diamond Match Company, Bryant & May had gained an interest in the Rosebank Match Company of Cape Town, one of the seven match manufacturers then operating in various parts of South Africa. The result of Bartholomew's visit was the formation, in 1905, of the Lion Match Company as a subsidiary of Bryant & May. This was an amalgamation of all the existing match companies in South Africa. Lion Match was the first of several overseas concerns that Bryant & May were to establish in the course of the following 25 years.

Leaflet c1904.

Another event in 1905 was the formation of the British Match Makers' Association, to combat the still increasing flood of cheap foreign matches into the British market. For 20 years the company had fought this problem by constantly bringing it to the notice of the government and the public. They urged the public to buy British matches, thus to give employment to workers at home at a time of severe depression. Again and again they had petitioned the government to control imports, but no effective action was ever taken. Thus seven of the principal United Kingdom manufacturers formed the Association for the purpose of safeguarding the common interests of all British manufacturers, and to regulate prices and production. The Association introduced a pooling system for home-produced matches through which each member was assigned a quota based on its normal deliveries of matches during the period 1897–1903.

The original members of the Association were Bryant & May, R Bell & Company Limited and J Palmer & Sons, all of London; W J Morgan & Company Limited and the Hulme Patent Advertising Match Company, both of Manchester; Paterson & Company Limited of Belfast and Dublin; and Maguire Miller Limited of Garston (near Liverpool) and Leeds. The Gloucester firm of Moreland & Sons Limited declined membership of the Association but agreed to co-operate in the pooling arrangements.

In 1906 the death occurred of Wilberforce Bryant at the age of 69 and 45 years after he had taken over the management of Fairfield Works. He had mainly been responsible for building the business into its leading position and establishing the name of Bryant & May throughout the world as producers of high quality matches. Although remaining active in the company up until his death, in later years he left the day-to-day management in the hands of Gilbert Bartholomew who, with George Paton, was to carry on the work of development and expansion. Wilberforce was the last of the Bryants to be connected with the business and on his death all that remained was the name.

His place as chairman was taken by his deputy (and one-time chairman of the British Diamond Match Company) William Alexander Smith, who held office until January 1908. He then handed over the chairmanship to the deputy chairman, Gilbert Bartholomew.

The death of Wilberforce Bryant did not affect the company's long-term plans for the expansion at home and abroad — plans which he had been mainly instrumental in forming. The first stage was the enlargement of the Bootle factory by one third and this extension was completed and opened in April 1909. Work then immediately started on building a completely new factory at the Fairfield Road site.

Unlike the Bootle works, which had been designed especially for modern match manufacturing, Fairfield Works had grown piecemeal since the buildings were converted to match making in 1861. Additions had been made as and when required so that by 1909 the site was a sprawl of buildings which was inefficient for the company's requirements. The new factory, constructed on a stage-by-stage basis, was completed and in full production by 1911, and employed some 2,000 women and girls. The new Fairfield Works, then the largest factory in London, was modelled on the Bootle factory but to a far higher standard. It remained a fine example for match factories throughout the world until well into the 1920s.

In both its factories, Bryant & May continued the policy concerning the health and welfare of the workpeople. Special attention was paid to the provision of the maximum of light, air, ventilation and heating. Kitchens and dining rooms served free tea and soup and a good midday meal at far less than cost price. A typical bill of fare of about 1912 survives:

Gilbert Bartholomew, chairman of Bryant & May 1908–11.

Cut from joint, potatoes and cabbage	$3d(1\frac{1}{4}p)$
Steak and kidney pie and two vegetables	$3d$
Fried fish and potatoes	$1\frac{1}{2}d$
Cold ham	$1\frac{1}{2}d$
Two rounds of bread and jam	$\frac{1}{2}d$

Other facilities for staff at this time included hostels for the matchgirls and a holiday home at the seaside resort of Colwyn Bay in Wales where as many as 60 girls at one time could be accommodated and fed at a charge of 10s 0d (50p) each a week.

Whilst development went on at home, important steps were

taken to extend manufacturing interests in overseas countries — especially in those where protective tariffs were affecting Bryant & May's export business. For more than a quarter of a century, the firm's most lucrative export markets had been Australia and New Zealand where, despite trade recessions and the impositions of import duties, business had steadily increased. In 1908, therefore, Bryant & May approached the Australian match-making firm of R Bell & Company with a proposal for amalgamation. R Bell operated a factory at Melbourne and another in Wellington, New Zealand. The proposal was accepted and, as a result, Bryant & May took over the two factories under the title of Bryant & May, Bell & Company (Proprietary) Limited of Melbourne and Bryant & May, Bell & Company of Wellington.

Cardboard capsules with sandpaper bottoms for wax-vestas. Between c1865–1910, they were made exclusively for the Australian and New Zealand markets. They were popular with gold miners for storing their gold dust or sovereigns, as the boxes were exactly the size for the latter purpose.

W A Smith retired from the company in 1908 and the position of chairman went to Gilbert Bartholomew. Under his leadership the company embarked on a long-term programme of widening the basis of its business. The plan was threefold: first, to acquire further interests in match making and importing both at home and abroad; second, to arrive at agreements with companies producing the raw materials and machines upon which the match industry depended; third, to diversify into activities other than match making so as to protect the company against foreseen and unforeseen vicissitudes in the match industry.

Over the years this plan proved an unqualified success, but its instigator and architect, Gilbert Bartholomew, was not to enjoy its fruits, for he died in December 1911 at the age of 59. Gilbert Bartholomew had come into Bryant & May from Bell & Black when the latter company was taken over in 1884, and he had been appointed general manager in the following year. His business activities were tireless and from the day he joined the company he added a drive to its affairs which was largely the cause of its high position in the match industry. In his private life he took a deep interest in hospitals, boys' clubs, municipal affairs and, above all, social work in the district where the factory stood. On the death of Gilbert Bartholomew, William Alexander Smith became chairman for the second time. His first task was the planning of a major scheme of diversification through acquisition.

The first step was the purchase in 1912 of the Bristol firework makers, Octavius Hunt Limited. This takeover was a good exercise in the practice of diversification as, like Bryant & May, Octavius Hunt were principally makers of hand-held lights — although in Hunt's case, these took the form of sparklers and Bengal lights.* The business was bought outright for £7,000 and continued its operations uninterrupted.

The following year the Gloucester match-making firm of S J Moreland Limited became a subsidiary. This company operated a factory which employed 500 people and was the maker of the still-famous brand of matches, *England's Glory*. In 1914, Bryant & May took over George M Judd & Brothers Limited, match makers of Stratford in East London. Then, in the same year, the company made its first entry into South America by acquiring an interest in the Brazilian match-making firm of Companhia Fiat Lux, de Fosforos de Segurança, founded in Rio de Janeiro in 1904.

By that time, the company had met the challenge of foreign competition at home through an intensive programme of rationalisation and modernisation whilst still strengthening its position abroad. That it had reached pre-eminence in the quality of its products was demonstrated in January 1912 by the award of the Royal Warrant as match makers to King George V which all his successors have renewed. Since the beginning of the century the company had trodden a path of continual progress. This was to be seriously checked — although by no means stopped — by the outbreak of the Great War.

World War I 1914–18

The first serious effect of the war on the British match industry was the cutting off of supplies of potash muriate, a German monopoly and one of the most important chemicals used in match making. Then as the war progressed, imports of timber became restricted through the shortage of shipping — so much so that the industry was threatened with a total shutdown.

George Paton, the managing director, immediately started a search for an alternative supply of potash muriate and found it in the ancient kelp industry of Scotland and Ireland where the chemical was produced from seaweed. For timber the company had to use whatever it could get. Almost as serious as the scarcities of raw materials was a rapid rise in prices due largely to steep increase in freight rates. In the case of timber these rates increased by 1,000 per cent while potassium chlorate, another essential ingredient, rose from 3d (1½p) a pound to 2s 3d (11½p) a pound.

Royal Warrant appointing Bryant & May as match makers to King George V.

*A firework with a vivid light used as a signal.

Fitzroy Collection

This famous and popular postcard by Bert Thomas illustrated the spirit of the typical British Tommy in his breaks from the horrors of the trenches in the Great War. The rights to the picture were subsequently purchased by Bryant & May and used for advertising.

Muriate of potash rose from £8 to £40 a ton. In addition to this, wages were increased with the institution of a wartime cost-of-living bonus of 3s 0d (15p) a week for all workers.

There were further difficulties in 1916 when the government imposed a duty of 4d (2p) on 1,000 matches. This was a heavy burden on the financial resources of companies like Bryant & May, for the tax had to be paid before the matches were sold. As was the case of the proposed match tax of 1871, the government introduced this levy without prior consideration of the consequences to the industry.

The immediate effect was that manufacturers were compelled to suspend the sale of matches because it was impossible to fix a price under the proposed method of calculating the tax due. After a series of meetings with government officials, the problem was eventually solved and the new retail price of matches fixed at three boxes for 2d — which was more than treble the pre-war price.

In 1917 the duty was further increased so that the price went up to 1d a box — at which it remained until the government, under the pressure of financing another war, raised the duty again in 1940.

The British match industry became faced with another challenge in June 1916 when, owing to the ever-increasing loss of shipping, the government totally prohibited the import of foreign matches. This step reduced the supply of matches by about one half and led to the great match shortage which was one of the minor features of the First World War — a shortage that demonstrated how essential the match had become both to industry and domestic life. For a time many people, lacking the means of fire making, became dependent on the old method of fire maintenance.

The shortage led to the placing of matches under the control of the Tobacco and Matches Control Board, the matches section of which was run by Clarence Bartholomew, then a director of Bryant & May. For his services, Bartholomew was awarded the OBE. Match manufacturers found that it was all they could do to try and narrow the gap between supply and demand. Consequently Bryant & May's output rose to a record level even though raw materials were still in short supply.

During the war the company produced special matches packed in damp-proof boxes to withstand the wet of the trenches on the Western Front. By arrangement with the War Office these were sent to France in tin-lined cases, each containing 1,008 boxes (one box for each man in a battalion). In other ways too, Bryant & May contributed to the war effort. In 1915 they presented a hut to the YMCA for the use of servicemen passing through Victoria station and lent their lorries from time to time to facilitate the movement across London of men on leave. The company donated large sums of money to the Red Cross and other war-time charities.

It is a tribute to the economic strength of the firm that not only did it pass through the vicissitudes of four years of war unscathed, but throughout the period it continued to expand. In 1916 the match-making firm of W J Morgan & Company Limited was acquired, and in 1918 work began on the building of a new match

Metal match-box case for use in the trenches 1914–18.

 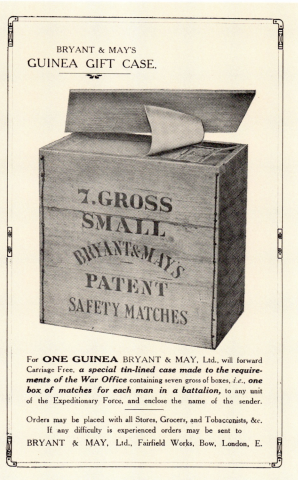

factory at Glasgow. This was to counter the severity of the match shortage in Scotland which was due mainly to transport difficulties. The first matches from Glasgow were produced in 1919 and in 1920 the factory was doubled in size. Other events that occurred during the war included the adoption of the trade name *Brymay* in 1916, and the formation of a Works Committee at Fairfield Road in 1918 — the first-ever body of its kind in Britain. Also in 1918, the company introduced a five-day week to offset the shortage of materials. This was found to be so successful that it was continued when normal times returned.

During the Great War 500 men and women from the company's factories served in the forces and this was a considerable proportion of the total labour force, especially as far as men were concerned. Of the latter, 65 were killed or wounded in action and 12 were decorated or mentioned in dispatches. Among these was Captain George Paton MC, the son of the managing director, who died in battle and was posthumously awarded the Victoria Cross.

'War Specialities' 1914–18.

The war had a profound effect on British industry. It involved government in production; it expanded productive capacity; it formed a more modern attitude towards labour; and all-in-all it set industry on a new path which was to lead by stages to the welfare state we know today. When peace came, Bryant & May, together with British manufacturers generally, had to face what amounted to another industrial revolution.

A Challenge 1919–27

As industry slowly returned to normal after the war ended it was challenged by the greatly increased powers of organised labour, for in 1917 the Whitley Councils had been instituted to destroy, almost at a stroke, the old concept of *laissez-faire*. Bryant & May accepted the challenge under the special influence of George Paton who, in 1918, had become chairman of the Joint Industrial Council for the match industry. Yet while adjusting to the new industrial situation, the company continued with its own long-established policy of improving working conditions. In 1919 a 47-hour week with full pay for Bank Holidays and a week's paid holiday every year was introduced.

Later in 1919 the firm started a co-partnership share scheme for its employees. 200,000 shares (each yielding 15 per cent tax free) were created to be acquired by staff from a bonus payable every year. The bonus was based upon the balance remaining from profits after eight per cent had been paid to holders of the company's ordinary shares. This scheme was the result of Paton's long-held belief that partnership between capital and labour was essential for industrial peace and national prosperity. Expounding this then novel idea to a meeting of shareholders he said:

> The only cure for this state of affairs [industrial unrest and strikes] is a partnership between capital and labour. Their interests, if not always identical in detail, are necessary to each other. I am constantly told 'Oh! co-partnership may suit your business — it is not possible in mine.' It's all nonsense; it can be adapted to any business. In some cases it is the employer who is afraid to part with something he has all along; in other cases it is the unions who fear loss of control of their members. In both cases, in my judgement, they are shortsighted. Co-partnership benefits both sides.

The introduction of the co-partnership scheme was closely followed by a non-contributory life assurance scheme for the benefit of the dependants of any employee who died. In 1921 a supplementary benefit scheme was started to protect staff from unemployment. These measures established Bryant & May as among the leaders of the progressive elements in British industry and it was this enlightened policy that helped to carry the company through the difficult years of industrial strife which were a feature of the post-war era.

Remembering the war-time shortage of timber, the company decided to try growing its own timber at home. In 1922 a 4,000 acre tract of land was purchased at Ballochyle in Scotland and planted

Early match-box advertising.

with aspen poplar for the making of match splints. A further 2,000 acres of land were acquired at Ballochyle in 1930. This first attempt at timber production did not come up to expectation and the estate was sold in 1960.

The expansion of the company's match-making interests continued. In 1922 the large match-making group of Maguire, Paterson & Palmer was purchased. This company owned one of the world's then most modern match factories at Garston near Liverpool and also controlled another large works at Leeds. Both these factories continued operations under Bryant & May and were expanded and modernised over the years following. The Garston factory, now greatly enlarged, is today the company's only British match factory and is still considered to be one of the most modern and efficient of its kind in the world. Various other match-making interests acquired in 1922 included the purchase of the Canadian Splint & Lumber Corporation and control of the Canadian Match Company of Pembroke. Overseas expansion continued over the following four years with the opening of new factories in Cape Town, Durban, Wellington and Melbourne.

Another important development in 1922 was the installation at the Bootle Diamond Works of the first continuous process machine for the production of book matches. These were first made in Britain at the Diamond Works in 1899 and during that year sales totalled 5 million books of 20 matches each. This figure must have been due to the novelty of the product for it was not maintained. Over the following 10 years sales never exceeded 2 million. Between 1910 and 1913 production again rose to 5 million but this trend was checked during the First World War. In 1918 production again rose steeply and in 1919 it was 8·5 million books.

Up to this stage book-match machinery was of American manufacture and composed of separate units as distinct from the continuous process machines used in the production of wood matches. Little was done to improve book-match making techniques because it was thought that book matches would never become popular. Consequently, although some improvements were made to existing machinery to keep pace with slowly increasing demand, the machines remained basically unchanged and production still involved a considerable amount of hand labour. But when it became evident that the demand was permanently on the increase, a continuous process book-match machine was produced. The adaptation of this machine at the Diamond Works was timely, for the overall British demand for book matches rose from 33 million in 1923 to 160 million in 1939.

In March 1926, Bryant & May Brazil was registered for the purpose of taking over the shares of Companhia Fiat Lux Match Manufacturers of Rio de Janeiro. This was a company with which Bryant & May had had financial and technical agreements since 1914 and the acquisition of its entire shareholding gave ultimate control to the UK company. In the following year a majority interest in the Eddy Match Company of Canada was acquired.

Book-match advertising grew into a large industry.

The British Match Corporation

British immunity from foreign competition which resulted from the war-time ban on match imports did not last long, for towards the end of 1919 the import of matches from Scandinavia was permitted. Over the following five years all import restrictions were lifted with the result that many new competitors joined Bryant & May's old foreign rivals in the United Kingdom. These included Finland, Czechoslovakia, Poland, Estonia, Lithuania, Russia and Italy — all in search of foreign currency. However, an increasing proportion of imported matches came from factories owned or associated by Swedish Match.

Match imports into Britain increased year by year until, by 1926, they totalled 10.7 million gross boxes and constituted a full 5 per cent of sales. This increase was largely due to heavy imports of Belgian matches. At that time Belgium was experiencing a period of severe inflation which created an illusion of substantial manufacturing profits, and in the course of a few years 15 new match factories went into operation in that country. In competition among themselves, Belgian manufacturers cut their prices severely and this had the effect of reducing the price level of Belgian matches in the United Kingdom to 5s 2d (26p) per gross boxes of 50 matches as compared to the average 8s 7d (43p) per gross for the British product. Other continental countries also used the British market as a dumping ground for matches. The effect of this was that the sale of the British product fell from 1.728 million boxes in 1921 to 1.310 million in 1926.

The sale of Swedish matches in the United Kingdom was also hard hit by continental dumping although this had little direct effect upon Bryant & May as a separate corporation, for it has imported no Swedish matches since the 1914–18 war. Nevertheless the company was indirectly affected and to explain the reason for this it is necessary briefly to trace the history of the Swedish match industry throughout the first quarter of the 20th century.

Following the success of the Lundström brothers' factory at Jönköping, a number of other match factories were started in Sweden, most of which achieved success. Gradually the need for rationalisation became clear and in 1903 the Jönköping company amalgamated with six others to form the Jönköping & Vulcan Match Company (which will be referred to as the Jönköping Group). A considerable number of other factories remained outside the group and in 1913 nine of them amalgamated as United Swedish Match Factories (the United Group) with a head office in Stockholm. This important merger was engineered by the financier Ivar Kreuger, then approaching the height of his powers and already the most influential figure in the world's match industry.

Kreuger was born in Sweden in 1879 and after a varied career in industry had established Kreuger and Toll, a firm of contractors upon which he built a vast financial corporation with ramifications in every part of the civilised world. As a result of the scarcity of

King George V, centre, with Queen Mary visiting Bryant & May's stand at the Wembley Exhibition in May 1924.

raw materials during the war, the Jönköping and United groups pooled their resources and later decided on a merger which resulted in the formation in 1917 of the Swedish Match Company with Ivar Kreuger at its head.

Before the formation of the Jönköping Group the various Swedish match manufacturers were selling their products to the United Kingdom through several importers. In 1903 Bryant & May obtained the sole agency in the United Kingdom for marketing matches of the Jönköping Group and to facilitate this a new British company, Match Agency Limited was formed, wholly owned by Bryant & May. This arrangement was continued until 1910 when the shares of Match Agency were transferred to the Vulcan Globe Match Company Limited, a British subsidiary of the Jönköping Group which then manufactured matches in its factory in the London borough of Barking. After the merging of interests of the Jönköping and United groups, the shares of Vulcan Globe were transferred to J John Masters & Company Limited, a firm founded in 1882 as importers of matches, mainly from Sweden. Through this merger, J John Masters acquired Vulcan Globe's London factory.

Thus in 1926 the sale of both home-produced and imported matches in the United Kingdom was dominated by Bryant & May and (through J John Masters) Swedish Match. In the face of the foreign competition which was steadily increasing both in volume and intensity it became obvious that the two companies must either collaborate or else embark upon a prolonged and exhausting competition in the markets in which they operated. Therefore discussions took place between Bryant & May, J John Masters and Swedish Match to find a way to achieve what every industrialist seeks — the economics of steadiness in supply and demand, and stability in price.

The negotiations resulted in the formation of the British Match Corporation Limited (BMC) with a capital of 6 million ordinary shares of £1 each, with the object of acquiring:

    a all the ordinary shares of Bryant & May Limited,

    b all the shares of J John Masters & Company Limited,

    c all the Swedish Match Company's interests in any business engaged in the manufacture or distribution of matches in the United Kingdom.

When the transaction was completed, Swedish Match held 1.8 million of the 6 million ordinary shares. Of the 12 original directors, eight were nominated by Bryant & May and four (including Ivar Kreuger) by Swedish Match. The board was chaired by George Paton.

The first business of BMC was to conclude an agreement with Swedish Match which covered the manufacture and sale of matches by both parties and their associates, both in the United Kingdom and overseas markets, whereby those markets were divided in

relation to the existing pattern of the parties' trade. The general effect of this division was to exclude BMC from all overseas markets other than the British Dominions and Colonies (outside Asia), Brazil, Columbia and the Argentine. Swedish Match were excluded from Canada and Brazil. Special arrangements were made for sharing trade in Australia and New Zealand. Bryant & May Limited, although nominally a subsidiary of BMC, maintained its independence as a manufacturer and continued to trade under its own name, as did Masters and its subsidiaries.

After the formation of BMC, Bryant & May and the Swedish Match Group agreed jointly to enter the Argentine market and approached Compañia General de Fósforos (CGF), then the leading Argentine match manufacturers, seeking a share in the company. When this request was refused, they secured a 50 per cent interest in a small Argentinian match company. This step made CGF think again and in 1929 arrangements were made to allow the participation of Bryant & May and the Swedish Match Group by the formation of Compañia General de Fósforos Sud America SA, which took over the match interests of CGF.

Expansion in the 1930s

Once freed from the necessity of competitively battling with its ally and friendly rival Swedish Match, the company turned its attention to deal with the still increasing threat of foreign competition and the rapidly worsening world-wide economic situation. It was in a strong position to do this, for at the time of the formation of BMC, Bryant & May owned or controlled numerous enterprises all over the world. At home it owned factories in London, Liverpool, Glasgow, Manchester, Gloucester and Leeds; in Australia, at Melbourne and Sydney with another under construction at Perth. It operated two factories in New Zealand and two in South Africa. In Canada it had cutting rights in half-a-million acres of forest land through its shareholding in the Canadian Splint & Lumber Corporation and owned a majority interest in the Eddy Match Company (acquired in 1927) which did 90 per cent of the match business in that country.

In South America it operated three modern match factories in Brazil and had a considerable interest in the Colombian and Argentinian match industries. Its other major interests included a 50 per cent holding in J & C Cox Limited of Edinburgh who manufactured high-grade glue and gelatine (both important ingredients in match making) and a holding in the tin box making firm of Jahncke, acquired in 1895 when wax-vestas were sold in tin boxes. There was also an interest in the important firm of Chambon Limited, printing machine manufacturers.

In addition to the combined effects of foreign dumping and world recession the company had other problems to face. There were for example the rapid increase in the use of electricity in the home and the greater use of the mechanical lighter. Both these had an ad-

Mechanisation at Fairfield Works, 1928.
OPPOSITE *Match making.*
ABOVE *Box making.*

verse effect upon the demand for matches at a time when British manufacturers were supplying only a half of the home demand and had much productive capacity standing idle.

The industry's troubles had been added to in 1927 by a new trade agreement between Britain and the Soviet Union which increased Russian match imports from a trickle to a flood at prices well below cost of production. The Russian matches sold wholesale at about 5s 6d (26½p) per gross boxes as against 9s 0d (45p) a gross for the British product. With import duty at 4s 4d (22p) a gross boxes, the Russians were therefore accepting 1s 2d (6p) per gross to cover production costs, transport and other charges. It is no less than astonishing that the British match industry was able to survive such devastating competition. That it did so was solely due to the superior quality of British matches — a quality which was recognised by the individual buyer who, in those days, would often ask for matches by brand name. Bryant & May were particularly fortunate in this respect, for some of their brands were household names. These included *Brymay Safety Matches*, *Puck*, *Captain Webb*, *Pilot*, *Pearl*, *Ruby*, *Bluebell*, *Bo-Peep*, *England's Glory*, *Swift* and, in particular, *Swan Vestas*. In addition to *Swan Vestas*, many of these old brands still exist.

Yet despite the difficulties that dogged the company throughout the depressed years, it continued to expand both at home and abroad. The Leeds factory was entirely rebuilt and modernised in 1932, and during the same year the firm of British Booklet Matches (1928) Limited was acquired. In 1933 further steps were taken to grow poplar for match splints by the purchase of 640 acres of land at Lakenheath, Suffolk.

Also in 1933 the Peerless Gold Leaf Company Limited was formed to exploit an American process for marking plastic containers. In 1935 a cautious diversionary move was made by the purchase of a majority interest in the British Basket & Besto Company Limited of Glasgow, makers of wood-veneer fruit packaging. In 1938, S J Moreland & Sons Limited became fully-owned. During the same period overseas, many factories were enlarged and modernised, whilst in South Africa, 800 acres of land were put under poplar for splint manufacture.

In 1937 Bryant & May launched out into Southern Rhodesia where a small but up to date factory was built at Salisbury. The reward for this bold expansionary policy under difficult conditions was recorded in the company's balance sheet which shows steadily increasing profits reaching £552,365 by 1939.

The Kreuger Crisis 1932

On 12th March 1932 there occurred an event that shocked the financial world and rocked the entire match industry to its foundations. This was the suicide in Paris of the financier, Ivar Kreuger, chairman of the Swedish Match Company and, it will be remembered, a director of BMC. At the time of his death this extraordinary

Popperfoto

The Match King. Ivar Kreuger, 1880–1932.

man controlled some 40 per cent of the world's match industry. The catastrophe and the long process of disentangling the complexities of Kreuger's business affairs was of such magnitude that it left a considerable legacy in the structure of the match industry which has lasted to the present day. At the time of his death Kreuger was 52 and at the climax of a career which, not confined to the match industry, had made him a giant in the world of international finance.

Kreuger was a financial genius almost obsessed with the idea of solving those world-wide economic problems which were causing such widespread misery. He fervently believed that by the exercise of free enterprise linked with intelligent co-operation between the financiers of the world, orderly economic progress could be assured. It might be said that his efforts were directed towards the same ends as the Bank of England, for together with the Bank, Kreuger and his immense financial organisation worked strenuously to restore the war-shattered finances of the Continent. It was his firm conviction that the key to the depression lay in the problems involved in the transfer of goods and cash, and that if these difficulties could be removed, the world's economic troubles would be resolved. To this end he was instrumental in obtaining a loan to Germany of the then vast sum of $125 million at a time when failure to obtain the money would have involved that country in catastrophe. He helped the French Premier, Raymond Poincaré, to obtain a stabilisation loan of $75 million when all other channels were closed. In these and other similar transactions, he acted for himself and his organisation and not as a representative of any government. From his own resources he made other loans to governments to deal with predicaments and emergencies.

A mere list of these cannot convey what his efforts really meant to the financially parched countries of Europe, but a few examples may be mentioned. He lent $6 million to Poland to rehabilitate flood-ruined farmers; $22 million to Yugoslavia for essential economic development; $36 million to Hungary for land reform; $6 million to Latvia to finance farm relief.

The money for these operations came mainly from Kreuger's enormous holdings in the world's match trade which, putting his faith in the internationality of industry, he had extended through one company after another. He provided for, and protected, his output by securing from governments the monopoly of their markets. These concessions he had to pay for in loans, and to finance these loans he was obliged permanently to mortgage all his interests to the maximum. But despite his theories and his efforts, economic conditions continued to worsen and governments did not always fulfil their financial obligations to him.

The resultant repercussions on his vast, yet intricate and delicate financial machine were disastrous and in 1932 Ivar Kreuger, seeing its inevitable breakdown, shot himself. When news of his death reached Sweden the cabinet was summoned, and within hours the Riksdag assembled to pass precautionary legislation to counter the catastrophe. Such was the impact of the death of this one man.

The stock of Kreuger's companies (especially those concerned with matches) fell by hundreds of millions of dollars almost overnight. Shares in his finance company, Kreuger & Toll (which had reached $46 a share in 1929), fell within weeks of his death to three cents. His personal liabilities alone amounted to an almost unbelievable $265 million, but this was as nothing compared to the $1,177 million which was claimed against his estate.

Ivar Kreuger has been much maligned since his death and, 50 years on, his name is still a byword for illegal and dishonest speculative operations. In fact he was a man who lived for the work which he so passionately believed would lead an ailing society back to economic health. In 1932 he had reached the peak of his career and if he saw only failure and frustration ahead, it must be remembered that he was broken in health and tired in mind after years of overwork. If he had a fault it was surely that he trusted too much in governments.

The 'Kreuger Crash', as it was called, had no effect on the affairs of BMC, for during Kreuger's five years' directorship of that company he had attended only two of its board meetings. Neither BMC or any of its subsidiaries (of which Bryant & May was the principal one) had any holdings of shares in Swedish Match or in any other company in Kreuger's group. Neither had BMC made loans to Kreuger companies, nor entered into any financial guarantees in regard to them.

The only way in which BMC was connected with the Kreuger débâcle was that Kreuger had, contrary to an undertaking given by Swedish Match, pledged part of the Swedish Match shareholding in BMC with a Stockholm bank as security against a personal loan — although, under the terms of BMC's formation, Swedish Match had undertaken not to part with possession or control of its shares in the British company without the latter's consent. No consent was given by BMC who, in fact, had no knowledge of the transaction. Thus the company emerged unscathed from a scandal which shocked and shook the world.

Sir George Paton

The success of the company during the worst years of the depression was due mainly to the business acumen and immense knowledge of the trade of two men; the chairman, Sir George Paton (knighted in 1930 for his outstanding public services) and Clarence Bartholomew (son of Gilbert Bartholomew), the deputy chairman. It was a serious blow to the company when Sir George died in March 1934 at the age of 75.

George Paton had joined Bryant & May as joint managing director with Gilbert Bartholomew in 1901 on the merger with the Diamond Match Company of which Paton was manager. In September 1924 he was appointed chairman of Bryant & May and, during his 10 years in office, he dominated the British match industry.

The company's rapid expansion under his leadership can be largely attributed to his foresight and firm belief in the development of the vast resources of the British Dominions. He was also a pioneer in the field of social benefits for the worker, and the wisdom of his attitude towards labour relations was demonstrated by the fact that none of the firm's factories was affected by the General Strike of 1926. Apart from his work for the company and the many advisory duties he undertook for the government, he devoted much time and thought to various charities — especially those concerning the youth of Scotland, the country of his birth.

Sir George Paton was succeeded as chairman by his right-hand man, Clarence Bartholomew — a man unrivalled for his knowledge of the international aspects of the match trade. In fact, Clarence Bartholomew had been personally responsible for the establishment of Bryant & May's wide interests in the British Commonwealth and Dominions. He had earned the OBE after the First World War for his services with the Match Control Office and in 1939 he received a knighthood for public services. Bryant & May were most fortunate in having a man of such outstanding ability and knowledge at such a time, for the Second World War was to present problems far greater than those of the earlier conflict. It was also to bring about unprecedented changes in the structure of the industry as a whole.

World War II 1939–45

By 1938 it was obvious that a Second World War was inevitable and Bryant & May, with the experience of the 1914–18 conflict behind them, embarked on a programme to accumulate stocks of essential supplies both for the home factories and for those of Australia and New Zealand. At the same time special investigations were carried out into methods of saving timber and finding alternative supplies. One step taken was the decision to import splints rather than logs from Canada thus saving shipping space.

The problem of finding adequate supplies of suitable timber for the Australian factories developed during the first year of the war. The match industry in Australia had imported its timber in the form of ready-made splints and box skillets (*ie* trays), but these supplies soon became almost unobtainable. The difficulty was overcome by securing supplies of local hoop-pine which was processed into splints and skillets in a new factory in New South Wales. This source of supply has continued ever since. In the last two decades hoop-pine has only been used for the production of outer boxes for Greenlites Waterproof matches. Bryant & May's Australian poplar plantations supply the timber for splints.

At home the result of the company's foresight was that there was no immediate dislocation in match production — in fact, factories actually stepped up output to an all-time record to meet the demand for matches resulting from the increase in smoking during the war. This increased production also helped to make up for the cutting off of imports from Scandinavia and the Low Countries, although

Clarence Bartholomew, chairman 1934–46.

small quantities of matches continued to arrive from India, Australia, Thailand and Portugal. But as the war progressed these supplies declined and the burden of supply fell almost entirely upon United Kingdom match makers. Early on in the war all large-sized boxes, fancy lines, individual coloured wrappings and coloured match holders were withdrawn — mostly never to return. The last wax-vestas to be made in Britain were produced at Bow in 1940.

To relieve the difficulties of distribution, the Match Control Board was revived as a department of the Board of Trade with responsibility for enforcing price control at trade and retail levels. It had a civil servant controller and secretary but the rest of the staff were supplied without charge by the match industry. Bryant & May provided most of these as well as the offices and facilities.

The Control Board was therefore exceptional among government agencies in being run by people who had a thorough knowledge of the goods they were controlling and of the firms with which they were dealing. It was run as an efficient business and its staff ensured that all applications were dealt with within 48 hours. The Board's chief executive officer was F H Dawson of Bryant & May who was awarded the MBE for his work.

One particularly heavy war-time burden was the continual increase in taxation, for then (as now) the British match industry was regarded by the Exchequer as an easy and ready source of revenue. In the first war-time budget the excise on matches was raised by $\frac{1}{2}$d a box, thus increasing the officially fixed retail price from 1d to $1\frac{1}{2}$d a box. Wages also rose steadily. Consequently, although production was at its highest in the company's history, profits declined from their 1939 peak of £552,365 to £399,706 in 1945.

The company was also seriously harassed by the grimmer aspects of modern war. Over a period of 11 months from August 1940 to June 1941, Fairfield Works suffered 13 direct hits and damaging near-misses from high explosive and incendiary bombs. But although various ancillary buildings were destroyed, the main factory remained practically unscathed. The remarkable feature of this period was that as a result of these incidents (some of which closed down the works for short periods) only 181 hours of work were lost. A more serious incident occurred in July 1944 when a flying bomb exploded in the factory yard causing the closure of the works for nine days.

The Spitfire fighter 'Swan', paid for by donations of Bryant & May employees from all over the world.

The biggest war-time disaster to befall the company was the total destruction of the Bootle Diamond Works on the night of 7th/8th May 1941, when a large number of incendiary bombs fell on the factory and set it ablaze from end to end. Although the destruction was complete no one was hurt. Most of the staff were transferred to the Garston site or other Bryant & May factories whilst the others had no difficulty in finding alternative employment. In any case, the company paid full wages to workers for any time lost.

It is a tribute to Bryant & May workers that they endured the ordeals of aerial bombardment with fortitude and good cheer and

All that remained of the Diamond match factory at Bootle after the German fire raid of 7th–8th May 1941.

whenever possible determinedly continued their work — a legacy, perhaps, of the *esprit de corps* of the original matchgirls. Together with their fellow-workers in New Zealand and Australia, they paid for a Spitfire fighter-plane (named *Swan*) which did valuable work before being shot down in July 1941.

After the German surrender the war ended with the detonating of atomic bombs on Hiroshima and Nagasaki in August 1945. This was fire far beyond the imaginings of those primitive humans who first learned how to make it. It ushered in a new industrial revolution, and a new world to which Bryant & May had to adjust.

PART THREE

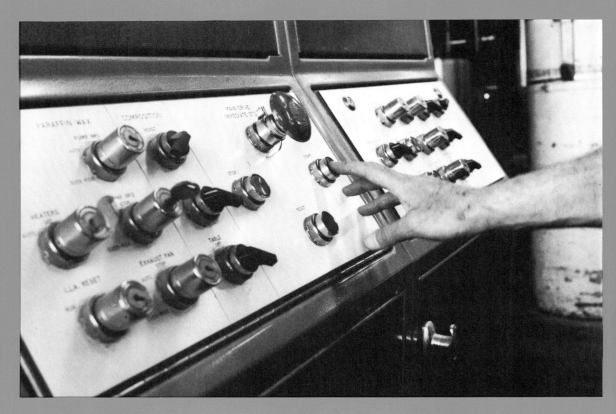

Making matches by automation.

THE AGE OF TECHNOLOGY

A Difficult Period 1946–49

The post-war period started badly for Bryant & May with the death, in 1946, of Sir Clarence Bartholomew OBE at the comparatively early age of 66. He had been a full-time director for 39 years and in this capacity had served longer than any other before or since. He was a boy of five when his father, Gilbert Bartholomew, became the company's first general manager, and as a youth he personally knew the Bryant brothers, sons of the founder of the business.

Together with his father and George Paton, Clarence Bartholomew had been a pioneer in the match industry with a wide and exact knowledge of the overseas side of the trade. Much of his time was spent in attending to company business in Australia, New Zealand, North and South America, Scandinavia, Germany and other parts of Western Europe. He seemed to be forever on a ship sailing somewhere and records show that he made 67 ocean voyages which totalled 245,500 miles.

Like his father he devoted much of his energy to charitable work, especially in the East End of London. It is no reflection on his successors to say that he was the last of the giants of the British match industry, for today increasing mechanisation dictates that managerial team-work is the key to success and there is little opportunity for the individual to dominate to the extent that he did in the past.

Sir Clarence Bartholomew was succeeded as chairman by Arthur Hacking CBE who had been a stockbroker and a barrister before joining Bryant & May in 1919. The problems he faced were formidable. Most of the war-time restraints were still in force. Raw materials and labour were still in short supply and the costs of them continued to increase: working hours were being reduced, wages and high taxation continued to rise. In fact, the after-effects of the war were, for a time, more serious than the war itself. The greatest problem was that of scarcity of materials which prevented the company going into full production at a time when matches were in short supply. There was ample timber available in Canada but it could not be purchased owing to the restriction of dollar-spending by the government. Other essential materials were strictly rationed, such as paper, board and glue. The company could not get enough glue for its needs even from its own glue-making factory.

Then, to make matters worse, came the bitter winter of 1946–47 accompanied by the great fuel famine of that year. This necessitated the temporary closing of the firm's small factories at Manchester and Leeds. Nevertheless, in this most difficult period Bryant & May continued to expand even though on a small scale. In 1948 a major interest was obtained in the Silver Fleece Steel Wool Company Limited of London and its selling agent, Joseph Stephenson & Company (London) Limited. Also at about this time an important step was made in the book-match business.

The destruction of the Diamond Works in 1941 had been a serious blow to Bryant & May, not least because of the loss of the company's entire book-match plant. In an attempt to preserve some contact with this highly competitive trade, three stitching machines and a comb-cutting machine were borrowed from Maguire & Paterson's Dublin factory and installed at Fairfield Works. Match combs were paraffined, dipped by hand, cut and stitched on the stitching machines and the result hand-packed. These efforts resulted in a small production of about 55,000 books a day, each containing 30 matches.

Soon after the war it was decided to step up book-match production by mechanising the manufacturing process, and designs were produced for a machine which could be incorporated with the continuous process wood-match machines at Fairfield Works. The designs for the new machine were produced by Bryant & May technicians and the machine was manufactured by Chambon Limited. By 1949 the company had three book-match machines in operation and three more awaiting erection. This demonstrated the company's long-formed ability to foresee the future, for from that year the demand for advertising book matches began a rapid and steady increase.

The still prevailing shortage of timber brought two important developments in 1949. One was the introduction of all-cardboard boxes for safety matches and the other (as a result of a government directive) a reduction in the size of most British matches. The wooden match became one-eighth of an inch shorter and slightly thinner — a change that involved complicated and expensive adjustments in match-making machinery. Other troubles during that year included another increase in the match tax which raised the retail price to 2d a box and, most serious of all, the government's decision to add further to the company's worries by referring BMC (British Match Corporation) to the newly-formed Monopolies and Restrictive Practices Commission — thus plainly implying that the company had acquired extraordinary powers.

The Monopolies Commission 1949

On 1st March 1949 the Board of Trade referred the first six selected industries to the Monopolies and Restrictive Practices Commission for investigation under the Monopolies and Restrictive Practices (Inquiry and Control) Act of 1948. Of these six, one was the supply and export of matches and one the supply of machinery for the manufacture of matches. The investigation was, in effect, into the affairs of BMC and its two active subsidiaries, Bryant & May and

J John Masters. The act defined a 'monopolist' as a 'person who supplies more than one third of any particular class of goods' and by that definition, Bryant & May had long been a monopolist. Of course, BMC could not be charged with any offence under the Act but the Commission's terms of reference clearly implied that the Corporation had used monopolistic powers without scruple and had grown rich and inefficient in the process. Having nothing to hide, BMC fully co-operated with the Commission, to the extent that for three and a half years the senior directors and executive staff of Bryant & May and J John Masters were burdened with preparing all the facts, figures and arguments required by the Commission. The Corporation believed that it had only to tell the truth in order to be fairly judged: in fact it was in for a shock.

The six industries chosen by the Commission were the first of many to be investigated and were, therefore, treated as subjects of experiment, for the Commission was new and its staff inexperienced. Furthermore, having little in the way of precedent to follow, they had to work out their own procedures and adapt their final conclusions and recommendations to an imprecise definition of the 'public interest'. With hindsight it is hard to avoid the conclusion that the Commission set out to search for any sort of skeleton in any kind of cupboard. Moreover, it rescinded two of its undertakings — that BMC would be told what evidence had been given by other parties, and that the company would be shown the report before it was published.

The report of the Commission was issued in May 1953 and ran to 135 closely printed pages. It was generally hostile to BMC and Swedish Match and the close relationship that existed between them. Among its conclusions it stated that:

i the absence of competition between manufacturers within the United Kingdom and between the United Kingdom manufacturers and the principal importers to this market has resulted in profits and prices being higher than they would otherwise have been, and at certain times this has also been true of costs.
ii the development of competition by independent British match manufacturers has been hampered:
   a by their being unable to buy machinery from manufacturers controlled by Swedish Match — the main source of supply in Europe — as they are in consequence of the agreements between BMC and Swedish Match;
   b by the practice which BMC has at times adopted in the past of temporarily underselling competitors in particular areas while maintaining the general level of its prices; and
   c by BMC's practice of charging its competitors higher prices for certain materials of which it controls the distribution
iii subject to the limitations imposed by the withdrawal in March 1952 of the Open General Licence for the import of matches, the decision as to what proportion of the United Kingdom market for matches is to be supplied from home manufacture and what proportion from imports rests, in effect, with BMC.
iv payments are made to Swedish Match as a method of reducing supplies of foreign matches to this country.

On 19th June 1953, Bryant & May sent to the Board of Trade a memorandum criticising the report where it appeared to be unfair. No reply to the memorandum was ever received. The main points it made were:

    a   The retail price of matches was 2d per box, of which more than half was taken by the Exchequer. The total price of 2d was accounted for as follows:

Excise duty	54%
Manufacturing costs	24%
Wholesalers' and retailers' margins	17%
Income and profits tax paid by manufacturers	3%
Balance for manufacturers' reserves and for shareholders' dividends	2%

    b   The revenue received by the government from the duty amounted to some £12 million per annum — *ie* nearly 40 times as much as the taxed profits of the manufacturers and importers.

    c   The average manufacturers' profit was about 1s 0d per 144 boxes. If profit were eliminated altogether the only reduction would be one penny a dozen boxes, which could not be passed on to the public.

    d   The British match industry was threatened with extinction by dumped imports in the 1920s and it was only by the building up of the industry by BMC that there were any matches to be had in the country during the war.

    e   The industry had provided a wide range of matches second to none in quality, had never created an artificial scarcity and had left the distributive trade free to buy where it liked and sell at what price it liked.

In its report the Commission had recognised that BMC in partnership with Swedish Match had a dominant position in the United Kingdom and that it was unlikely and unrealistic that either would want to destroy a partnership which had 'lasted so long and with such favourable results'. The Commission had also agreed that in most match-producing countries monopolies were formed and that was probably the natural organisation for the match trade.

As a result of the report the Board of Trade recommended that the partnership between BMC and Swedish Match should be allowed to continue although without 'objectionable features', namely the quota and oversales arrangements for the United Kingdom market; the partnership, it said, was desirable in the national interest and valuable with regard to technical assistance.

To the two companies involved it seemed highly undesirable that an end should be put to their internal arrangements for regulating the British match market — arrangements which did not affect the trade of other manufacturers and imports, let alone consumers. It also seemed unreasonable that they should be asked to collaborate wholeheartedly in everything pertaining to manufacture and overseas markets, while competing unrestrictedly in the United Kingdom match market. In the end good sense prevailed and a new trading agreement with Swedish Match was entered into in March 1954.

In the new agreement the earlier arrangements concerning quotas and compensation were eliminated and there was no provision for sharing the United Kingdom market. Neither was there restriction on the expansion of United Kingdom manufacturing capacity or the sales of either company's production. BMC's overseas interests, which were secured by the earlier agreement, were preserved.

The agreement was eventually approved by the Board of Trade and no significant changes to it have since been made. The extent to which BMC emerged from the enquiry with a clean sheet may be judged from the fact that when the new Restrictive Practices Act became law in 1956, the BMC group had not a single restrictive agreement to register.

Planning Ahead 1950-54

In 1950 the timber shortage still prevailed and considering perhaps that it might last forever, the company purchased 517 acres of woodland at Great Marston in Herefordshire.

Another change in match production came about in 1951 when the Board of Trade amended price control on matches to allow the same price per box to be charged but with reduced contents — 47 instead of 50 for ordinary matches, and 95 instead of 100 for *Swan Vestas*. At the end of the year price control was lifted and, after 20 years, the match industry was free to manage its own affairs.

This gesture of *laissez-faire* was, however, followed by another when the government in 1955 lifted all restrictions on the import of foreign matches. Most of the imports that resulted were from Western Europe and were fair competition but, on the abolition of quotas, Russia again began dumping large quantities of matches on the British market at prices that were slightly less than Bryant & May were paying for raw materials alone. Taking stock of the situation, the company realised that if it were to continue with its pre-war plan of expansion and widespread diversification it must find ways of making the best possible use of its resources, materials, plant, labour and capital. Thus BMC embarked on an intensive five-year plan, part of which was the setting up in September 1955 of a Diversification Committee under the chairmanship of Sir Anthony Elkins.

Diversification 1955-71

Ever since the end of the Second World War it had been realised

that the match industry had to a large extent become static. The reasons for this were that whereas by forceful sales campaigns and promotions people can be persuaded to buy more food, drink, detergents and the like, they will only buy as many matches as they need for lights. Whilst the increase in population greatens the number of match users, this increase is offset by competition from other flame-kindling devices — notably mechanical pocket and domestic lighters. There was, and is, an increase in the demand for matches in the developing countries where standards of living are rising, but even in those areas electrification may rapidly and substantially reduce the need for matches by curtailing the use of oil lamps, primitive cooking devices *etc*.

It was the static situation in the industry that had decided BMC in 1955 to embark on a long-term programme of expanding into new interests both at home and abroad. This important decision was justified by Sir Anthony Elkins at a seminar at the London School of Economics in 1963:

> Diversification, in recent years, has been much in evidence throughout industry, and from time to time it has attracted criticism particularly from those who hold the view that if a company has no further scope for expansion in its own field, it should hand surplus funds back to its shareholders, thus allowing them to decide in what other sorts of enterprise they would like to re-invest their money ...
>
> In our own case we found ourselves in a position in which our basic industry had become static for reasons quite beyond our control, and to have accepted the thesis would, I am sure, have been detrimental to our shareholders' interests ... We are industrialists, not financiers.

Sir Anthony Elkins CBE, chairman 1955–64 during which period he motivated the company's expansion programme.

The first business of the Diversification Committee was to concentrate on the acquisition of concerns which had some affinity or connection with the group's main activities so that not only money but knowledge and experience could be contributed to the new interests. The fields chosen were wood products; printing and packaging; pyrotechnics, and forestry.

The group was experienced in all these fields. It made woodveneer punnets for the soft-fruit trade and wooden boxes for flowers; it had interests in the printing and packaging business; it made sparklers and Bengal lights; it had forestry interests both at home and abroad. Following the recommendations of the committee, the company wasted no time in embarking on an expansion programme which, for speed and diversity, has few parallels in British industrial history.

The first move took place in 1956 with the closure of the Leeds factory and the transfer of its work to Garston. In the same year it acquired three firms concerned with printing and packaging — the Wolverhampton Box Company Limited, makers of plain and fancy cartons; Print & Paper Limited of Burton-on-Trent, manufacturers of coloured drip-mats and cellulose layer-pads, and the century-old Luton firm of C A Coutts & Company Limited, makers of cardboard containers. A major acquisition made in December 1958 was that of the Airscrew Company & Jicwood Limited which made

OPPOSITE *Feature in a Pains-Wessex firework display over the River Thames.*

Poplar growing in Australia. Part of the Bryant & May estate in Yarrawonga, Victoria.

wood chipboard and other waste-wood products. Airscrew at the time operated factories at Weybridge and Annan, and Bryant & May later added two more — one at Marks Tey and another at Hexham. From that time all Bryant & May's wood waste, formerly burnt or sold very cheaply, went to Airscrew for conversion into board. Also in 1958, a major interest was purchased in Prestfibre Limited, and its subsidiary, Pimfibre Limited — both makers of moulded woodpulp products. The involvement in packaging was further developed in 1959 by the acquistion of the high-quality carton manufacturing company, H W Chapman Limited of Wellingborough.

In the field of pyrotechnics, the group acquired two companies engaged in the manufacture of fireworks, marine rockets and smoke pesticides. First of these (in 1960) was the famous Mitcham firm of James Pain & Sons established in the 17th century. The other (acquired in 1963) was Waeco Limited of Salisbury. In 1965 Pain and Waeco were amalgamated under the title Pains-Wessex Limited.

Considerable expansion was also made in forestry through the purchase in 1955 of an estate in Norfolk and another in Bedfordshire. Overseas the company added to its timber growing in South Africa and Canada and embarked on poplar growing in Australia, Brazil and the Argentine. These developments were aimed primarily at producing timber in areas adjacent to the match-making factories in the countries concerned. To consolidate the timber-growing activities, a new company, Bryant & May (Forestry) Limited, was formed in 1961.

Overseas expansion and diversification during this dynamic period included the acquisition of three Australian companies — Tamco Pty Limited and Mahlco Plastic Industries Pty Limited, both producers of precision mouldings, and Field Instruments Pty Limited who make metal fittings for small boats. In the field of match making, the Eddy Match Company of Canada became fully owned, as did the Federal Match Company of Sydney. In 1963 the company opened a new match factory in Recife, Brazil, which was acknowledged to be one of the most modern of its kind in the world.

Concurrent with the diversification programme was a five-year, £1.5 million plan which provided for large-scale modernisation of the company's factories at London, Liverpool and Glasgow. The result of this was the improvement of automation to the extent that today it takes only an estimated seven seconds of human labour to produce each box of matches.

At the close of this energetic decade the group was in a strong position. It consisted of the holding company, British Match Corporation Limited: a main subsidiary and principal operating company, Bryant & May Limited: the J John Masters Group, primarily responsible for the sale of the Swedish Match Company's products, and Bryant & May (Latin America) Limited which held the group's considerable interests in the match industries of Brazil and other Latin-American countries. In addition there were some 58 subsidiary and 'sub-subsidiary' companies and nine associated companies operating in twelve countries in all six continents. The manufacture of matches was still the group's main interest both at home and overseas and it accounted for 75 per cent of its total asset value and 81 per cent of its gross profits. It was on the virtual completion of the diversification and modernisation plans in 1964 that the driving force behind them, Sir Anthony Elkins, resigned as chairman of the Diversification Committee and of Bryant & May. He was chairman of the British Match Corporation from 1964 until his retirement in 1972, and in that position continued to exert a powerful and beneficial influence both on the international match business and on the other diversified businesses of the Corporation. Sir Anthony Elkins was succeeded by Ian Gilbert.

Throughout the 1960s the expected decline in match demand continued, both at home and abroad, and as a result the decision was made in 1971 to close the factories at Bow and Glasgow and to confine United Kingdom match-making operations to the Liverpool works. Over the following years production at Bow was gradually transferred to Garston; on its closure the Fairfield works employed only 275 people — a far cry from the days when thousands streamed through the gates. In 1979 the machines stopped for the last time. Match making in London's East End was finished and Bryant & May's last remaining link with its origins was broken. In 1981 the Glasgow works was closed and the Garston factory remained as the only producer of wooden matches in the country.

Pistol by James Wilkinson c1810 and trade card of James Wilkinson & Son c1820.

Wilkinson Sword – Wilkinson Match 1973

After the success of the diversification programme and the period of consolidation which followed, it appeared to the board of BMC that considerable advantages for world-wide market growth would be gained if a merger were to be arranged with another international manufacturing group — one which, in its products, the people it employed and the skills it represented, would benefit both parties. Essentially, the organisation sought after was one whose reputation for quality of products and service matched BMC's own.

After considerable research into this proposition, the seemingly ideal partner for such a merger was found in the old-established company of Wilkinson Sword Limited, manufacturers of razors, razor blades, shaving systems, men's toiletries, hand and power garden tools, fire extinguishers, fire protection systems — and swords. This range of products fitted perfectly with that of BMC — as did Wilkinson's marketing organisation and areas of activity. At the time of the merger, Wilkinson Sword employed 3,439 people and had a turnover of £24,303 million.

Wilkinson Sword had been founded in 1772 by Henry Nock in Ludgate Street near St Paul's Cathedral. Nock made several types of gun, including sporting guns and rifles, duelling and target pistols, personal defence pistols, blunderbusses and military weapons. In 1792 he received a government contract for 10,000 muskets and bayonets — the largest order ever placed up to that time by a

Wilkinsons are still famous for their finely-wrought swords and make them for important ceremonial occasions. Here a modern Wilkinson craftsman is polishing the basket hilt of a broadsword.

British government. Nock also made ordnance pieces, a field in which he was a great innovator. In 1802 he became Master of the Worshipful Company of Gunmakers and, in 1804, received the Royal Appointment as gunmaker to King George III. Since that time the company he founded has continuously held Royal Appointments as gun- or sword-makers to the British Sovereign.

Henry Nock died in 1804 and his partner and son-in-law James Wilkinson inherited the business, continuing to enhance its reputation for best quality workmanship and innovative design. James's only son, Henry Wilkinson, became a partner in the company in 1820 and he took over full control in 1825. Henry moved the business to 27 Pall Mall (conveniently next door to the offices of the Board of Ordnance) and here he continued to make fine military and sporting guns and also swords. Like his father and grandfather, Henry Wilkinson produced many notable improvements and novel designs for firearms. He also took a keen interest in swords and brought his inventive mind to bear on the problem of improving quality and performance. His military swords soon became famous for strength and balance, and sword making became an important part of the business. By 1887 the company was concentrating wholly on swords and changed its name to The Wilkinson Sword Company Limited.

By the turn of the century Wilkinson Sword had begun to diversify into other products. Its first razor (the *Pall Mall*) appeared in 1898, to be followed by typewriters, bicycles, motorcycles and a wide range of sporting and hunting equipment. The *Pall Mall* razor, with its stroppable single-edged blade, was developed into the famous *Empire* razor of 1929 featuring a built-in automatic stropping device. This model continued in production until 1948 and many are still in use.

In 1920 the manufacture of garden tools was begun, and in 1934 the company turned to aircraft fire-protection systems, which activity developed into marine and industrial applications.

On the outbreak of the Second World War, Wilkinson Sword returned to the production of military equipment (which included fire-protection systems for the Royal Air Force). After the war it reverted to making razors and gardening equipment while still manufacturing fire-protection systems for aircraft, marine and industrial applications. In 1956, the company entered the double-edge 'wafer' razor-blade market and in 1961 marketed the polytetrafluoroethylene-coated 'Super Sword Edge' blade. This innovation led to a large expansion of blade production, which rose from 50 million blades in 1961 to 500 million in 1964 — the year in which Wilkinson Sword became a public company.

The next major step was the introduction in 1971 of the Bonded Shaving System — a single-edged blade held in a frame at the optimum angle and protusion for shaving. Further diversification came about in 1973 when the company acquired a controlling interest in the European operations of Scripto Incorporated of America, which makes a wide range of writing instruments. At the

Production at Garston today. Punch-out section of modern 12-box movement match line.

Book-match combs in drying chain.

Fiat Lux labels 1910–20 and today.

time of the merger with BMC, Wilkinson Sword had subsidiary companies and bases in Germany, USA, Canada, New Zealand, Italy, France and South Africa and its products were selling in over 100 countries.

The amalgamation of BMC and Wilkinson Sword produced a single group employing 15,500 people with a turnover of over £100 million. The organisation which resulted from the merger did not replace the existing corporate structures of the two groups; rather it overlaid them in a way that preserved the identities and traditions of both. BMC became Wilkinson Match Limited, and as such is the parent company to Wilkinson Sword and its various subsidiaries, whilst still retaining the original BMC interests. These include Bryant & May, which continues to operate independently under its own name.

In 1980 ownership of Wilkinson Match was wholly acquired by the US firm of Allegheny International Incorporated, a Pittsburgh-based company which serves world-wide markets with an extensive range of consumer goods and industrial specialities, in many respects similar to those of Wilkinson Match and its subsidiaries. This merging of interests proved to be of considerable benefit to both parties, for it provided wider marketing outlets for Allegheny while substantially broadening the Wilkinson product range. As a result of this development, Bryant & May became part of the Allegheny group, although this change in the proprietorship of the company did not in any way affect its structure or management.

The Company Today

It is now 142 years since the firm of Bryant & May was founded, and 124 years since it produced its first matches. Today the company is still concerned primarily with the making of lights and, operating on a world-wide scale, produces and markets no fewer than 340 billion matches a year.

The company's central and most profitable operation is in the United Kingdom where, at the Merseyside works, 36 billion matches are manufactured yearly. This represents 54 per cent of the entire British match market. This powerful position is due to the steady demand for a range of standard match brands led by *Swan Vestas* (which holds 25 per cent of the total United Kingdom market), followed by *Brymay* in the south, *England's Glory* in the Midlands and the north, and *Scottish Bluebell* in Scotland. Recently this list of famous brands has been augmented by the introduction of *Cook's Matches*, in large boxes containing 280 matches for general use around the house and garden. A very substantial investment in the Merseyside works is currently being made to improve productivity and to maintain Bryant & May's world leadership in the quality of its products.

Although the United Kingdom is the company's most profitable market, it is by no means its biggest in terms of output. This distinction belongs to Bryant & May's Brazilian subsidiary, Fiat

Lux, whose annual production amounts to 146 billion. This is 60 per cent of the total Brazilian market and represents almost half the group's total output. The reason for the enormous consumption of matches in Brazil is that some 90 per cent of that country's population of 121 million rely on butane-fired stoves for cooking. In Brazil, the group has four match factories and two splint plants using timber drawn from the State of Parana in the south and from the Amazon Forest in the north. Fiat Lux also has its own timber plantations, both in the north and the south of the country and it is the long-term plan eventually to use only plantation timber for match production in Brazil.

The second largest producer in the group is the Lion Match

Match boxes today – including classical and modern designs for both National and regional sale. Box striking surface and label are made and printed in a single operation.

TOP *South African labels, old and new.*
ABOVE *Lion label c1900.*

A Redhead label of 1940 and the label today. In the latter, the Redhead subtly implies flame.

Company of South Africa, with an annual output of 67 billion. Since being formed by Bryant & May in 1905, Lion Match has moved from strength to strength and now supplies 99 per cent of the still-expanding South African market. Lion has two large factories, each with its own integrated splint plant. It also has manufacturing units in Zimbabwe, producing seven billion matches a year, and Malawi making four billion. Lion Match also has a factory in Mozambique which, through a good working relationship with the government, supplies the entire Mozambique demand of four billion matches a year.

The Eddy Match Company of Canada has also grown considerably since Bryant & May's first investment in 1902. Now wholly owned, Eddy supplies 50 per cent of the Canadian market with an annual production of 12 billion. 90 per cent of this output is in the form of book matches which are very popular in Canada. This is the only substantial market in book matches with which Bryant & May is closely connected.

In Australia, Bryant & May have two factories producing between them 13 billion matches a year. The company also has a range of magnificent plantations centred on northern Victoria and a modern splint factory situated alongside its biggest plantation at Yarrawonga. In 1972, the Australian operation was extended to Papua where a small match factory was established which now produces two billion matches a year and accounts for 60 per cent of the Papuan market. Bryant & May keep a careful watch on the Australian consumer market, for it is there that new ideas and trends tend to become taken up and later spread to other parts of the world. It was in Australia that disposable lighters first found a large market and in consequence it was one of the first territories to which the company introduced the item.

In New Zealand the company continues to flourish. The factory acquired in 1908 was destroyed in an earthquake in 1972 and replaced by a new, attractive works situated just outside the capital. Today this unit supplies 99 per cent of the New Zealand market which (as a result of the rising popularity of disposable lighters) demands only three billion matches a year. The group recently acquired a minority interest in the Polynesia Match Company of Western Samoa and also the total equity shareholding in Pacific Manufacturers Limited, which dominates the Fijian match market. Managed from the head office of Bryant & May New Zealand Limited at Upper Hutt near Wellington, these two firms produce just over half a billion matches a year.

For many years, Bryant & May held a 33 per cent interest in the Irish match-making firm of Maguire & Paterson Limited which has a small but well equipped factory in Dublin. In 1981, the group acquired 100 per cent of the company, making it a fully-owned sister company to Bryant & May. The main reasons for this move were to use the full potential of Maguire & Paterson in distributing a range of consumer products in Ireland, and to consolidate the dominance of Bryant & May in the Irish lights market as well as

Production in Australia. Final inspection of finished match boxes.

that of the United Kingdom. With an annual production of six billion matches, Maguire & Paterson has an 80 per cent share of the total Irish match market based on its two major brands, *Cara* and *Friendly*. The company is also distributor of Wilkinson Sword products in Ireland as well as a number of other consumer products.

Sales of the Group's overseas operations now far exceed those of Bryant & May in the home market. This is a legacy from the early efforts and extensive travels of Gilbert Bartholomew and his son Clarence which established the company's great tradition of worldwide investment.

In 1977, Bryant & May made a tentative entry into the disposable lighter market in Australia. This was a timely move, for the modern form of 'tinder box' soon became popular all over the world, and Bryant & May became established as a leading distributor of disposable lighters in many of its territories. It should be stressed that the company is still only a distributor of lighters, for it makes none of its own. Its function is to sell lighters alongside matches, thus preserving and widening its role as a major supplier of lights.

To supply the Australian market, the company imports lighters and sells them under the names of *Redlights* (to reflect the name of its popular *Redheads* matches) and *Citylights*. Today these brands have 22 per cent of the considerable Australian market for disposable lighters. In South Africa, the Lion Match Company entered into the market with a low-priced disposable lighter. Then, in 1983, it launched a high-quality disposable lighter which is sold alongside the cheaper model. Together these two lighters command more than 20 per cent of the South African disposable lighter market. Bryant & May entered the UK lighter market in 1981 and offered two disposable lighters under the brandnames of *Chukka* and *Clix*, and a 'refillable disposable' named *Clipper*. Although the

Gripper chain receptacle for Redhead matches.

UK lighter operation is only four years old, it has already achieved a 35 per cent share of the inexpensive lighter market.

In 1984, Bryant & May moved into a new related market through the introduction of a range of smokers' requisites. This comprises lighter fuel, gas-lighter refills, lighter flints and pipe cleaners. A consumer research programme had shown that no brandname dominates the marketing of these items and thus there exists no brand loyalty. It was decided therefore to promote the range under the name of *Swan*, a strong brand image that is known to at least 99 per cent of smokers in the UK. Much thought was put to the packaging and presentation of this small but comprehensive range, and there can be no doubt that it will become the smoker's main choice. An important advantage to the retailer is that, for the first time in the UK, matches, lighters and related items are now available from one supplier.

Ever since its beginnings the firm of Bryant & May has grown steadily — not in size alone, but in every industrial and commercial dimension. The factors behind this growth are many and various and may be summarised as follows. First, the company has always been capable of forecasting and correctly evaluating the changes in demands in its particular field. Second, it has always kept abreast of the far-reaching mechanical and engineering advances that have changed the face of industry during the past 125 years, and adapted to those advances through constant modernisation of plant and machinery. Third, it has always kept the quality of its products high on its list of priorities and thus built and preserved a first-class brand reputation. Fourth, the company has always been fortunate in having dedicated, skilled management at all levels to carry out planning, control and improvement in all departments of all its units.

Last, but by no means least, Bryant & May have always been acutely aware that a company is a collection not only of land, buildings and machinery but, above all, of people, and that good management-staff relationship is an indispensable factor in any business enterprise. In this respect the company has many 'firsts' to its credit. It has always been deeply concerned for the health of its people and was a pioneer in improving staff welfare and working conditions at a time when these were in sore need of reform. It was also among the first to introduce a co-operative scheme and a pensions plan for its workers. This productive alliance between industrial progress and staff welfare may be said to have been founded in 1861 when the business acumen of William Bryant was united with the benevolence of Francis May, and which formed the basis of the company as it is today.

OPPOSITE *'The yellow swan famous and agreeable.' (John Lydgate c1430.) The historical development of Swan labels.*

Having led the market in smokers' lights for 100 years, Bryant & May introduced a range of smokers' requisites in 1984 under the brand name of Swan.

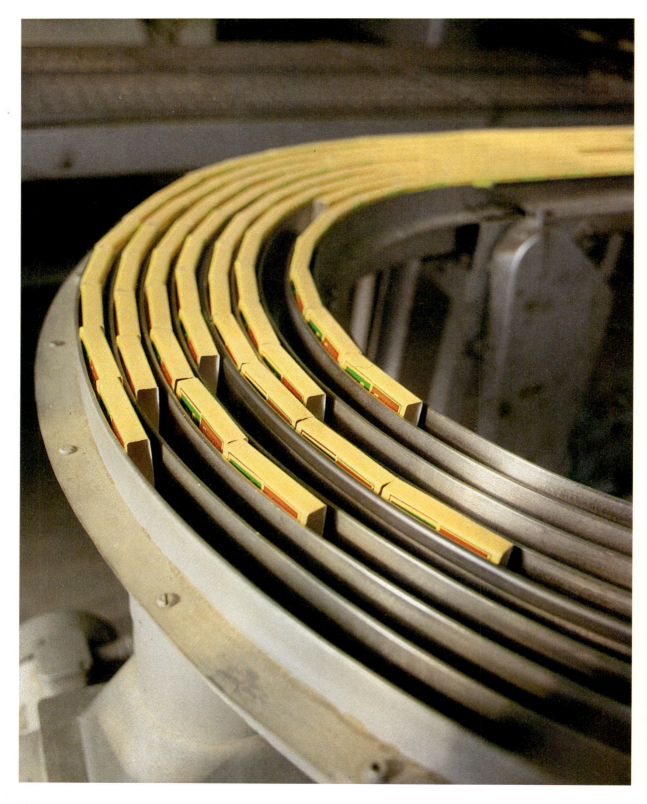

SWAN VESTAS 1883-1985

A 'vesta' (after *Vesta*, the Roman goddess of the hearth and household) is defined as a 'kind of short match, especially with a wax shaft'. The first recorded use of the term occurs in Catherine Sinclair's novel, *Holiday House* (1839). 'Laura afterwards singed a hole in her muslin frock while lighting one of the Vesta matches.'

Swan Vestas were first introduced by the small Bootle matchmaking firm of Collard & Kendall in 1883. They were made of cotton wick dipped in wax (like short lengths of taper), were pure white in colour and much more solid than other wax matches then available. The box depicted a swan almost identical to that used today, floating on a pond with lilies in the background.

When the Diamond Match Company took over Collard & Kendall in 1895, it continued the manufacture of wax *Swan Vestas*, but two years later introduced a 'sister brand' called *Swan White Pine Vestas*. This was a wooden match with a round splint, important for a smoker, for a round match burns better in the open air.*

Swan White Pine Vestas were made of selected and matured pine and manufactured on Diamond's then revolutionary 'cut-set-and-dip' machines. The new brand was marketed alongside the original wax *Swan Vestas*, its purpose being not to compete with the old brand but to capture the popular market for wax matches. From the beginning *Swan White Pine Vestas* made a strong impact on the match market and by the 1930s was Britain's best-selling match: so it is today, for it is the only British match that is consistently asked for by name. Sales of *Swan Vestas* represent half of Bryant & May's match turnover in Britain, and claim 28 per cent of the total British match market. The reasons for the continuing success of *Swan Vestas* are simple. They have a long-established reputation for quality; both box and design have unique features which distinguish them from ordinary matches and, most important, the user of *Swan Vestas* does not risk running out of lights nearly as soon as the users of other matches.

When Bryant & May amalgamated with Diamond Match in 1901, the production of *Swan Vestas* was continued at Diamond's Bootle factory and an intensive advertising campaign at once launched to promote the brand. In 1906 the words *White Pine* were dropped from the actual brandname and transferred to the back of the box to be replaced with the slogan, 'The Ideal Match for Smokers' (later shortened to 'The Smoker's Match'). When the change from round to square splints happened, the description *White Pine* was dropped and the Royal Warrant took its place.

*Round *Swan Vestas* continued to be produced until 1952 when they gave way to square splints as part of a modernisation programme.

TOP *'It pays to advertise.'* The company sold this seaside postcard, with appropriate resort names, all over the country.

ABOVE *Shop display card c1910.*

OPPOSITE *Finished boxes coming off production line.*

Filled Swan inners and outers prior to assembly.

From 1890 *Swan Vestas* were sold in a variety of sizes of containers. The first, known as 'No 8' *Swan Vestas*, was a flat cardboard box printed in red (sometimes mauve) on a white label. This was followed in 1900 by the 'No 12' box which bore the red, green and yellow design which is used today. The 'No 15' box was double the length of the 'No 12', while the 'No 18' contained two rows of matches side by side. Then in 1912 the 'Knapsack Box' offered *Swan Vestas* in a metal container with a spring lid — a line much in demand by soldiers during the First World War. In about 1914, *Royal Swan Vestas* were introduced.* These, the most impressive of all Bryant & May products, were matches with a 'bird's eye dip', *ie* each had a yellow tip on variously coloured heads of green, red, maroon and blue. According to the firm's copywriter of that time, these glamorous lights had 'the added dignity and sophistication of being packed in svelte, flocked boxes with gold leaf lettering.'

Together with all other fancy matches and packagings, *Royal Swan Vestas* were withdrawn at the start of the Second World War

---

*Bryant & May marketed a *Royal Wax Vesta* (with a bird on the box) as early as 1876. It was probably with this in mind that Collard & Kendall introduced *Swan Vestas* named after the Royal bird.

as industry concentrated on the war effort and rationing was introduced. Reintroduced in 1958, they met with little success and were soon withdrawn. Between 1920 and 1933 Bryant & May marketed *Dainty Swan Vestas* ('For My Lady'). These tint-headed matches were sold in packets of one dozen boxes, each box of a different design and colour.

Since being acquired by Bryant & May, *Swan Vestas* have always been widely advertised and promoted. In 1902 a free case of four gross 'No 8' *Swan Pine Vestas* packed in patent tin boxes was presented to any retailer who ordered five or more cases of *Puck* or *Captain Webb*, two popular match brands then manufactured at the Diamond Bootle factory. A novel and most effective promotion mounted between 1914 and 1917 featured a free accident life insurance policy inserted into every box of *Swan Vestas* like a coupon. The main condition of the insurance was that a box of *Swan Vestas* had to be found on the injured person at the time of the accident, and that death had to be due to injuries sustained whilst travelling.

'Give-away' items and 'special offers' have appeared on *Swan Vestas* boxes from the early days. These included a photographic printing outfit for children, a wallet for servicemen, ashtrays, tablemats, football and cricket fixture lists in the form of boxes of *Swan Vestas*, a large variety of puzzle books, and a range of match containers. In more recent times special offers have included a wide range of items which includes propelling pencils, pens, key rings, aprons, playing cards and peppermint rock.

When first introduced in 1883 the price of a box of 100 *Swan Vestas* was one penny ($\frac{1}{2}$p) and remained thus for over 30 years. Then, on the introduction in 1916 of the first match tax, the price was increased to $1\frac{1}{2}$d for 75 matches. For nearly 15 years this price was maintained but, owing to a doubling of the tax in 1940, the price was officially fixed at 3d ($1\frac{1}{4}$p) for a count of 100. Mainly because of further tax increases, the price has risen steadily since 1949, from 4d per 100, through a series of variations in that count, until 5d (2p) for 96 was reached towards the end of 1962. Surprisingly, this price was held throughout nine years of escalating inflation until the introduction of decimal coinage in February 1971, when a new count of 65 matches was sold retail for 2p — this being the nearest equivalent of the old price of 5d. This was followed in June by a 3p box with pro-rata count increase to 98. VAT and rising costs have since increased the price by stages until today when a box of 90 *Swan Vestas* costs 10p.

The factors that have contributed to the ever-increasing popularity of *Swan Vestas* are the convenient size of the box, the size of the match, the attractiveness of the label and, above all, the brand's unparalleled reputation for reliability. If in some future time matches are completely superseded by more up-to-date flame-kindling devices (as once was the tinder box) there can be no doubt that *Swan Vestas* will be the last survivors of an old, essential industry.

A change of course. Until 1959 the Swan swam to the left. It then changed direction.

Rickards

MATCH MAKING TODAY

Automation

Although it is difficult to compare the complex, automated operations of Bryant & May's Merseyside works with those of the old Bow factory in the early days, it is a fact that after 124 years of continual technical development, the basic processes involved in making and packaging matches remain substantially the same.

Match making is a classic example of mass production, and an essential factor is a stringent system of quality control. In match making it starts at the timber plantation and finishes with the inspection of the boxed matches. More than 50 materials go into the making of a box of matches and each ingredient is tested on arrival at the factory. Further checks are made throughout the manufacturing processes.

The wood used must be of the finest quality for its particular purpose: it must be white, odourless, straight-grained and sufficiently porous to absorb paraffin wax. To meet these requirements, Bryant & May makes its splints from aspen (also known as wild poplar). A single aspen tree yields an average of two million splints, and for each of the 12,000 trees felled each year, a replacement is planted. The wood is grown and cut into splints in Canada and delivered to the Merseyside works — now the only wood-match factory in the United Kingdom.

On reaching the factory floor the splints are automatically placed into individual holes in the steel endless belts of machines which pass them through baths where their ends are soaked in hot paraffin wax before the match heads are applied. The wax helps the match to burn by transferring the flame from the head to the stick, for without it the match will go out as soon as the combustible matter in the head is burnt. Next, the belt takes the splints over a metal trough containing the liquid ignition composition and the heads are lowered to pick up the required amount. Some 6,000 splints at a time are dipped and as they are raised each stick carries a drop of the composition to form the striking head.

The preparation of the ignition composition is perhaps the most exacting process in match making and is carried out with scientific accuracy: for the way a match strikes — its efficiency, reliability and safety — depends upon the delicate balance of the chemicals constituting its head. The composition of the head differs according to whether a match is of the safety or strike-anywhere variety. The safety head contains potassium chlorate and sulphur, which ignite on contact with the amorphous phosphorus in the striking surface on the box. Strike-anywhere match heads are composed of potassium chlorate and phosphorus sesquisulphide, which combine to form a mixture that ignites when rubbed against a rough surface.

Drum buffer storage system for match-box covers.

OPPOSITE *Modern match line: control panel and final inspection area.*

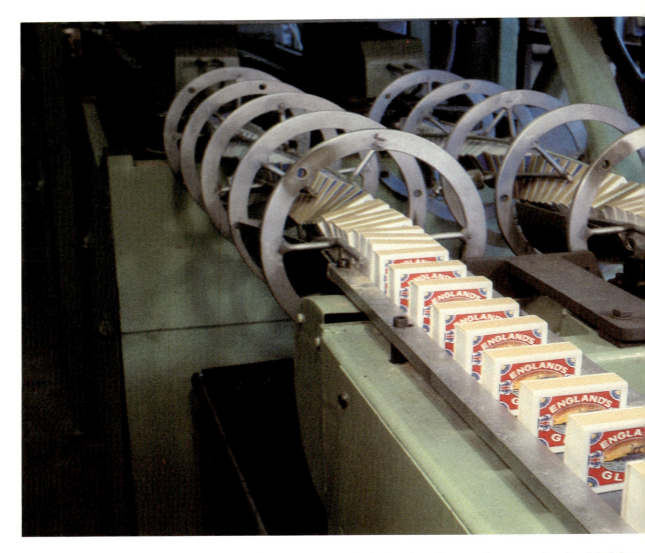

After receiving their heads, the matches are slowly dried by being carried through the machine for about an hour: then the belt takes them down to meet the inner boxes which move at right angles across its path. At this point the matches are automatically punched out of the belt to fall in the correct quantities into the moving inner boxes. The full inner boxes are then carried to a parallel moving belt holding the outer boxes, and are pushed into them. Each machine repeats this operation 50 times a minute to produce 800 fitted boxes per minute. The finished boxes of matches are then automatically gathered into a variety of packagings to suit the various retail outlets.

As we have seen, Bryant & May pioneered the use of box-making machinery, and thus the abolition of the sweated industry of match-box making by hand. Today the company continues to make all its own boxes at the Merseyside works. The paper board from

Out-feed end of modern sanding unit.

which both inner and outer boxes are made is stored in large reels, each weighing half a ton. To make the outer boxes for strike-anywhere matches, the board is fed into a machine which prints at a rate of two miles an hour. After being left to dry for two or three days, the board is fed into another machine which makes it into boxes and applies the striking surfaces. This is composed of a mixture of glue and graded sand, blended with citric acid which cures the glue and forms a hardened surface. The completed outer boxes then travel through a series of graded heaters which dry the striking surfaces. This machine produces 900 boxes a minute and feeds them into a hopper which channels them into the match-making machine.

Outer boxes for safety matches are similarly produced, but on a machine which prints the labels and applies the striking surfaces in one continuous operation. The outer boxes for *Cook's* brand

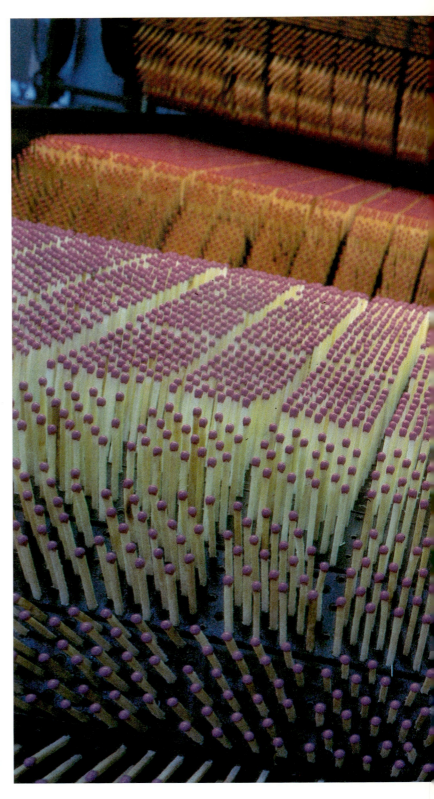

'Technology made large populations possible; large populations made technology indispensable.' (Joseph Wood). Woodstick matches in drying chain.

Rickards

matches have a varnished finish which is printed by H W Chapman Limited, one of the group's subsidiaries. They are delivered to the Merseyside works where the striking surface is applied. The inner boxes for all Bryant & May brands are made by machines which cut, form and glue in one operation.

Envoy

This history appears at a time when industry as a whole is undergoing technological changes, the ultimate effect of which will be as drastic as those of the first industrial revolution, and there can be no doubt that these developments will eventually produce new production methods which, as yet, can only be imagined. The directors and management of Bryant & May face these changes with the same confidence that has assured the firm's progress ever since the day in 1860 when the founders decided to make their own matches.

Bryant & May is justifiably proud of its past achievements, as also of the fact that it is prospering in the present. But the company is aware of its future too and, to this end, is fully committed to a multi-directional course of action. It will continue to improve the quality of its products to ensure the preservation and further enhancement of a reputation which has, in the UK at least, made its name synonymous with matches. It will pursue its fight against the ever-present threat of foreign 'dumping' of cheap matches: as in the past, this will be achieved through product development, plant modernisation and efficient management.

Finally, it will seek out and exploit other products related and complementary to its existing trade, thus utilising to the very limit the marketing experience and distribution strength built up over the last 124 years.

BRYANT & MAY CHAIRMEN   1884-1985

Wilberforce Bryant	June 1884– February 1906
William Alexander Smith	March 1906– January 1908
Gilbert Bartholomew	January 1908– December 1911
William Alexander Smith	December 1911– August 1924
George William Paton	September 1924– March 1934
Clarence Edward Bartholomew	April 1934– March 1946
Arthur Hacking	April 1946– December 1952
Joseph Henry George Reed	January 1953– March 1955
Sir Anthony Joseph Elkins	April 1955– September 1964
Ian Herbert Gillett Gilbert	September 1964– March 1972
Robert Lewis Charles Stuart	April 1972– March 1973
Geoffrey Rae Smith	April 1973– March 1976
Christopher Walter Kemp Saunders	March 1976– September 1981
John Anthony Bloxcidge	September 1981– March 1982
Richard Henry Armitage	April 1982–

INDEX

Airscrew Company & Jicwood 105–06
Allegheny International Incorporated 110
Australia 60, 62, 75, 81, 91, 95–6, 99, 106, 112–13

Bartholomew, Clarence 84, 94–5, 99, 113
Bartholomew, Gilbert 61, 70, 75, 79–82, 99, 113
Belgium 88
Bell & Black 61–2, 81
Bell, R. & Company 79, 81
Besant, Annie 64, 67
Bluebell Matches 92, 110
Book matches 87, 100, 112
Booth, Charles 64
Bo-Peep Matches 92
Boyle, Robert 18
Brand (alchemist) 18
Brazil 82, 87, 91, 106, 110–11
British Basket & Besco 92
British Booklet Matches 92
British Match Corporation 88 *et seq*, 94, 100–3, 105–8, 110
British Matchmakers' Association 79
Bryant & May (Brazil) 87
Bryant & May (Forestry) 106
Bryant & May (Latin America) 106
Bryant, Arthur 38, 61
Bryant, Frederick 38, 61, 70
Bryant, Theodore 38, 66
Bryant, Wilberforce 38, 46, 52, 61, 75, 79–80
Bryant, William 21, 23–7, 29–30, 33, 38, 41, 43, 46, 52, 62, 115
Brymay Safety Matches 92, 110

Canada 87, 91, 95, 106, 112
Canadian Match Company 87
Canadian Spint & Lumber Corporation 87, 91
Captain Webb Matches 74, 92, 119
Cara Matches 113
Carkeet, Henry 61
Chambon 91, 100
Chapman, H.W. 106, 126
Children (employment of) 39 *et seq*
China 60
Coignet Père & Fils 33
Collard, Kendall & Company 74, 117
Compañia General de Fósforos 91
Congreves 21, 43
Cook's Matches 110, 123
Coutts, C.A. 105
Cox, J&G. 91
Czechoslovakia 88

Dainty Swan Vestas 119
Dawson, F.H. 96
Diamond Match 60, 74 *et seq*, 79–80, 87, 94, 96, 100, 117
Diversification Committee 103 *et seq*
Dixon, E.M. 61
Dobereiner, Johann 19

Eddy Match Company 87, 91, 106, 112
Elkins, Sir Anthony 103, 105, 107
England's Glory Matches 82, 92, 110
Estonia 88

Fabian Society 64
Fairfield Works (Bow) 37–42, 46, 52, 56, 64, 66, 69–72, 75, 79–80, 85, 96, 100, 107, 121

Fawcett, Millicent Garrett 71
Federal Match Company 106
Fiat Lux 82, 87, 110–11
Field Instruments Pty 106
Finland 88
Fire Making (early) 13, 15 *et seq*
Friendly Matches 113
Fusees 35

Garston Works 79, 87, 96, 105, 107, 110 121–3
Gilbert, Ian 107
Gladstone, William 47, 50–1, 66, 67
Glasgow Works 85, 106–7
Greenlight Waterproof Matches 95

Hacking, Arthur 99
Haukwitz, Godfrey 18
Hulme Match Company 79
Hunt, J.S., & Company 61
Hunt, Leigh 64
Hunt, Octavius 82
Huntley, Bourne & Stevens 56

India 60, 62, 96
Ireland 60, 112
Irish Match Company 75
Italy 88

Jahncke (tin-box makers) 91
James Pain & Sons 106
Japan 60
Jones, Samuel 21
Jönköping Group 88–9
Jönköping Match Factory 24–7, 33, 36, 38, 40, 42, 88
Judd, George M., & Brothers 82

Kreuger, Ivar 88–9, 92 *et seq*

Lighters (mechanical) 16, 91, 105, 112–14
Lion Match Company 79, 111–13
Lithuania 88
London Trades Council 66, 67
Lowe, Robert (Chancellor of Exchequer) 47, 50–1
Lucifers 21, 38
Lundström, Carl 24–30
Lundström, Johan 24, 26–8, 30, 33, 36–7

Maguire Miller 79
Maguire & Paterson 112–13
Maguire, Paterson & Palmer 87, 100
Mahlco Plastic Industries Pty 106
Malawi 112
Masters, J. John 89, 100–01, 106
Match (invention of) 13, 17fn, 18 *et seq*
Match Agency 89
Match-box making 42–3, 62, 122–23
Matchgirls' Strike 64 *et seq*
Match Tax Battle 47 *et seq*
May, Francis 21, 23–6, 28, 30, 38, 41, 43, 46, 62, 115
Monopolies Commission, 100 *et seq*
Moreland & Sons 79, 82, 92
Morgan, W.J., & Company 79, 84
Mozambique 112

New Zealand 62, 81, 91, 95–6, 99, 112
Nock, Henry 107

Pace & Sons 61
Pacific Manufacturers 112

Pains-Wessex 106
Palmer, J., & Company 79
Paterson & Company 79
Paton, George 75, 79–80, 82, 86, 89, 94–5, 99
Pearl Matches 74, 92
Peerless Gold Leaf 92
Phosphorus 18, 21, 38–40, 43, 70–2, 121
Phosphorus necrosis ('phossy jaw') 21, 35, 70–2
Pilot Matches 92
Pimfibre 106
Poincaré, Raymond 93
Poland 88
Polynesia Match Company 112
Prestfibre 106
Print & Paper 105
Puck Matches 74, 92, 119

Quakers (Society of Friends) 23, 56

Recife Works 106
Redhead Matches 113
Restrictive Practices Act 103
Rosebank Match Company 79
Royal Swan Vestas 118
Ruby Matches 74, 92
Russia 88, 92

Safety matches 28 *et seq*, 38, 42, 70, 121
Shaw, George Bernard 67
Silver Fleece Steel Wool Company 100
Smith, William Alexander 80–2
South Africa 79, 91–2, 112–13
South America 82, 87, 91, 99, 106, 110
Southern Rhodesia 92
Spitfire (Swan) 97
Stead, W.T. 64
Swan Smokers' Accessories 115
Swan Vestas 74, 92, 103, 110, 117 *et seq*
Swan White Pine Vestas 117
Swedish Match Company 89, 91–2, 94, 101–3, 106
Swift Matches 92

Tamco Pty 106
Tiger Matches 74
Timber growing 86–7, 103, 106, 111–12
Tin boxes 43, 56–7
Tinder box 16
Tobacco and Matches Control Board 84, 95–6
Trummer, Otto 61

Union of Women Match Makers 64, 67
United Group 88

Vesuvians 35, 43, 52, 70
Victoria, Queen 47–8
Vulcan Globe Match Company 89

Waeco 106
Walker, John 19 *et seq*, 28
Wax-vestas 43, 52, 70, 96, 117
Webb, Sidney 64
West Indies 75
Wilkinson, Henry 108
Wilkinson, James 108
Wilkinson Match 107 *et seq*, 113
Wilkinson Sword Company 107 *et seq*, 113
Wolverhampton Box Company 105

Zimbabwe 112